From
PRODIGAL
To
PRIEST

"Fr. Goyo Hidalgo gives us the story of his own life—a modern-day experience like that of the prodigal son. It's a message that will fill everyone who comes across it with hope and a clear understanding that God will always embrace us with open arms, no matter who we are, no matter what we've done, and no matter how long we've been away. And if our modern world needs to hear one message above all others, it's precisely that."

Tommy Tighe
Author of *St. Dymphna's Playbook*

"Fr. Hidalgo's witness allows us to reflect on the power of our own stories and how God calls each of us as the prodigal son. This book leads us to reflect honestly on how God is working in our daily lives and how to cultivate a rich life of prayer. Fr. Hidalgo highlights the peace that Christ alone can give us and invites us to a daily 'yes' to God working in our lives."

Adam Cross
The Catholic Therapist

"Fr. Hidalgo's joy radiates in this book, inviting us all to reflect on our own stories of conversion and transformation. Fr. Hidalgo never fails to make me smile every time we're together, and this book is like sitting down with my dear friend and hearing his story from start to finish, knowing that Jesus is with him, and me, throughout it all. This book, and Fr. Hidalgo, are gems, and you will love both."

Katie Prejean McGrady
Host of the *Ave Explores* podcast and
The Katie McGrady Show on SiriusXM

"Here is an inspiring story of a prodigal's journey of faith from a 'far country' to the grace of conversion and Holy Orders. Discover God's fatherly love and patience—and the power of a loving mother's prayers—from Fr. Hidalgo's honest, joyful, and humorous account. Highly recommended."

Scott Hahn
Catholic theologian

"This book, simply yet powerfully written, will prove helpful to anyone who feels lost, anyone who knows that there is more to life than wealth and pleasure, anyone who is sincerely seeking God. You will be drawn in by Fr. Hidalgo's personal story, and through it you will learn some of the most important principles of the spiritual life."

Bishop Robert Barron
Diocese of Winona–Rochester

"The fastest and surest way to the heart is vulnerability. From the first page of *From Prodigal to Priest*, Fr. Goyo Hidalgo's vulnerability and willingness to share his journey had me ready to listen with an open heart. That listening led to laughter, tears, and a deep desire to love Jesus Christ more. I am so grateful for this book as I know it will cause you to know, love, and serve the heart of our loving and merciful Lord. Read this book, pray with it, and then share it. It will change lives!"

Fr. Rob Galea
Singer-songwriter, speaker, and author of *Breakthrough*

"Fr. Goyo Hidalgo tells a great story with a powerful lesson: sin does not get the last word in anyone's life. Our Father's forgiveness and compassion are open to everyone, no matter what we may have done or how far we may have fallen away from him. I pray that this book will help many people find their way back to the Father's house and know the embrace of his mercy and love."

Archbishop José H. Gomez
Archdiocese of Los Angeles

From PRODIGAL *To* PRIEST

A Journey Home to Family, Faith, and the Father's Embrace

FR. GOYO HIDALGO

Ave Maria Press AVE Notre Dame, Indiana

Founded in 1865, Ave Maria Press is a ministry of the United States Province of Holy Cross.

www.avemariapress.com

Paperback: ISBN-13 978-1-64680-212-8

E-book: ISBN-13 978-1-64680-213-5

Cover art of "Luke 15:11–32 The Parable of the Prodigal Son" by Daniel Profiri / 2DBox, www.etsy.com/shop/2DBox. Used with permission.

Cover city image © 4kodiak.

Cover and text design by Samantha Watson.

Printed and bound in the United States of America.

Library of Congress Cataloging-in-Publication Data is available.

Without my parents' prayers and their love for God, I would not be who I am today. This book is fruit of their exemplary lives. I miss them both, especially my mom's lessons on how to love God.

To my sister Ana, you sacrificed all for me and I love you very much.

To Penny and Carmen, wonderful friends who always supported me. I am blessed to know you.

You know the moon is beautiful.

This book would have never happened without my editor, Jayme. Her encouragement, patience and wisdom are out of this world. I pray for you every day.

To all my brother priests. I am always encouraged by your sacrifices and hard work. I pray for you always.

To all prodigal sons and daughters, never lose hope. God is always waiting for you.

Parable of the Prodigal Son

Then Jesus said, "There was a man who had two sons. The younger of them said to his father, "Father, give me the share of the property that will belong to me." So he divided his property between them. A few days later the younger son gathered all he had and traveled to a distant country, and there he squandered his wealth in dissolute living. When he had spent everything, a severe famine took place throughout that country, and he began to be in need. So he went and hired himself out to one of the citizens of that country, who sent him to his fields to feed the pigs. He would gladly have filled himself with the pods that the pigs were eating; and no one gave him anything. But when he came to himself he said, "How many of my father's hired hands have bread enough and to spare, but here I am dying of hunger! I will get up and go to my father, and I will say to him, 'Father, I have sinned against heaven and before you; I am no longer worthy to be called your son; treat me like one of your hired hands.'" So he set off and went to his father. But while he was still far off, his father saw him and was filled with compassion; he ran and put his arms around him and kissed him. Then the son said to him, "Father, I have sinned against heaven and before you; I am no longer worthy to be called your son." But the father said to his slaves, "Quickly, bring out a robe—the best one—and put it on him; put a ring on his finger and sandals on his feet. And get the fatted calf and kill it, and let us eat and celebrate; for this son of mine was dead and is alive again; he was lost and is found!" And they began to celebrate.

Now his elder son was in the field, and as he came and approached the house, he heard music and dancing. He called one of the slaves and asked what was going on. He replied, "Your brother has come, and your father has killed the fatted calf because he has got him back safe and sound." Then he became angry and refused to go in. His father came out and began to plead with him. But he answered his father, "Listen! For all these years I have been working like a slave for you, and I have never disobeyed your command; yet you have never given me even a young goat so that I might celebrate with my friends. But when this son of yours came back, who has devoured your property with prostitutes, you killed the fatted calf for him!" Then the father said to him, "Son, you are always with me, and all that is mine is yours. But we had to celebrate and rejoice, because this brother of yours was dead and has come to life; he was lost and has been found."

—Luke 15:11–32

CONTENTS

INTRODUCTION

Since becoming a priest, I have met many people who are not happy with their lives. They are looking for answers—like I once did—in alcohol, parties, drugs, relationships, and being constantly entertained by the world. But when all of that stops and they find themselves in loneliness, reality takes them back to being unhappy again. Many have asked me to help them find happiness and have even cried out to God. But the journey home is not clearly mapped out in front of us, and most don't know how to begin.

In this book, I share my journey back to the Father. The joy and difficulties. The yearning for understanding and silence before God. The tears of shame and the joy of forgiveness. All of these are part of my story. I don't know if they are part of yours. But I do know that if I made this journey home, anyone can. The steps might not be the same for everyone, but the loving Father who longs to embrace us happily runs out to meet every one of us.

I hope I can help you or someone you know find the way home to the God who loves you. I did not make the journey alone, and you don't have to either. Whoever you are, whatever you have done in your life—even if you think that it is unforgivable—when you are at the end of the rope, or find yourself in a pigsty, be not afraid. God knows you.

God loves you. God wants to forgive you, and he is waiting for you with open arms.

Prayer of a Prodigal

Father,
I don't know how to talk to you
Or if you will even listen to me,
But I am here because the voices of the world
Were stronger than your whispers.
But now that I am alone and tired,
I remember when I walked with you,
When my heart was full of joy.
I desire to come back to you,
But I am scared and full of shame.
I don't know what to do or say,
But I know I need you.
The noises of the world are painful
And so are my sins, my choices, and my lost
    journey.
Father, please let me come home
Because I am homeless and without love.
I need you and your love.
Amen.

1

ONE APRIL MORNING

But when he came to himself he said, "How many of my father's hired hands have bread enough and to spare, but here I am dying of hunger!"
—Luke 15:17

I woke up on that April morning like I did on so many other days. I was half-naked, a bit sick, and the TV was still blasting. I had come home after another night of partaking in alcohol with friends—my way of mitigating my pain and masking the fact that deep inside I did not like my life. I had many days like that—in fact, a decade like that. It was 2005 and for the previous ten years all I had done was work, buy everything I wanted, and go out every night hoping to meet someone who would make me happy enough to feel that my life was worth something. I never thought about how long that happiness would last, but hoped it would last for at least a little while. A day, an hour was all it would take to keep me going.

On that morning I never suspected how different things were going to be. I had come home drunk and lain on my couch, regretting my choices and wishing to forget the day.

It took me a while to get used to the light in my room, but after a minute, the words "Be not afraid" flashed across the TV screen. They didn't mean much to me then, but I had a feeling that something was happening.

As I sat on the couch and saw those words, I suddenly felt awake, maybe more awake than I had ever been. "Be not afraid." I kept looking at the words on the screen. I wasn't sure who was telling me not to be afraid or why, but I wanted to know. And for the first time in a long time, I was interested in something beyond myself.

The broadcast turned out to be live coverage of the funeral of Pope John Paul II. I was familiar with him, of course. I had grown up in Spain, part of a very devout Catholic family. Faith was an important part of my childhood. The memories were clear and strangely peaceful, so I kept on watching. I really couldn't look away. I so wanted to not be afraid—but I wasn't even sure what I was afraid of.

I turned up the volume and watched attentively. After a few minutes of looking for an easy way to find peace, I found tears. Suddenly, it was as if I was really present before God. I felt naked. In a long second, I saw myself at my worst and I was totally ashamed. Then, with my hands covering my face, I began to cry loudly.

Then something happened to me. I saw my whole life. My youth full of happiness, my years in minor seminary. The wonderful years with the youth group in my little town. Childhood prayers with my mother. The religious festivals of the patron saints of my town. Going to Mass with my parents. I saw it all. It was so intense and so vivid. My whole life was in front of me, revealed in just a single second.

There I was, ugly crying, almost breathless, when a terrifying thought surfaced in my brain: my mother. What was I going to tell my mother? If I told her about what I had done over the past ten years, it would break her heart. I had always loved my mother more than anyone in this world, and I didn't want her to see her son like this. Her faithful son, the one who wore the white suit she made for First Communion and sang so beautifully at the end of Mass. The son who wanted to be a priest. The son who loved going to youth retreats and was so happy to celebrate Holy Week and sing in the church choir. What happened to him? What happened to me?

I don't know if you have ever asked yourself those kinds of questions, or maybe know someone who has. It is a difficult place to be because the answers are not simple or easy but complicated and painful. They show us the ugliness and pain of our life. They also show us how very far we can travel from all that is familiar and good without ever intending— or deciding—to do so. It doesn't happen overnight or all at once. More often than not, we move away from God slowly, without even realizing it.

On that morning, I understood that I was like the prodigal son in the Bible. I had left home, not just physically but spiritually, and had squandered everything my family had given me. I was almost literally in a pigsty, and I was starving to death. In that moment, I knew what I was hungry for. I wanted—and needed—to return to my family, my faith, and my heavenly Father. Was it possible to come home? I didn't know. What I *did* know was that if there was a way, I had to find it.

The good news is that there is a way home. It is a way many before us have taken, one we do not have to walk alone. The path begins wherever we are when we come to our senses and realize how far we've fallen, how unhappy we are, how empty our lives have become. That happens only when we take the risk of being honest with ourselves. When we look around us and see where we really are, we can no longer stay there. And when we look within us and see who we've become, we know that only God can help us. And he will.

Prayer of a Prodigal

Father,
I don't know how to talk to you
Or if you will even listen to me,
But I am here because the voices of the world
Were stronger than your whispers.
But now that I am alone and tired,
I remember when I walked with you,
When my heart was full of joy.
I desire to come back to you,
But I am scared and full of shame.
I don't know what to do or say,
But I know I need you.
The noises of the world are painful,
And so are my sins, my choices, and my lost
    journey.
I have come to my senses, Father.
Now, please let me come home
Because I am homeless and dying of hunger.
And I know now that I need you and your love.
Amen.

2

A RICH INHERITANCE

*The younger [son] said to his father, "Father, give
me the share of the property that will belong to
me." So he divided his property between them.*
—Luke 15:11–12

Anybody can end up in a pigsty. My childhood was filled with
faith, love, laughter—and a hint of poverty. And yet, I wasn't
too sad about not having much. It was all because Mom knew
how to make a lot out of nothing. While we never had many
material things, our family was rich in faith. Everything about
how we lived came from that treasury.

Mom was generous with those who had even less than we
did. Once she asked me to find my three best toys. I wasn't
sure what she was going to do with them. Maybe play with
me? Looking at me with love and firm determination, she
said, "Pick your favorite toys. We are visiting someone very
poor today, and you are going to give those toys to their children." I wasn't happy about this at all. Then she kneeled in
front of me and said something I never forgot: "Your best is
not what you have but what you give. Giving something you
love the most is your best."

Mom's mission in life was to teach us everything she knew about God, Mary, and the saints. And oh, how she loved those saints! Every day we heard a story of a different saint, but Mary was probably her favorite. We had a statue of Mary in almost every room of the house, and Mom told us every day to love Mary more than anyone. "If you don't love Mary more than you love me, then you don't love me the right way." Mom never studied theology, but she had all kinds of theological one-liners that could shake your heart.

At the time, the constant reminders of God's love might well have gone over my head. But Mom planted the little seeds anyway. Evangelization came easy to her because she was not afraid of what people might think. I, however, was a bit embarrassed. My intellectually disabled younger brother made my friends uncomfortable. So, Mom would let me play with my friends on the street, then in late afternoon she used to open the door and shout, "Kids, I have chocolate and milk!" We'd run to the house, and Mom would be there in the living room with a tray of chocolate and glasses of milk on the table. Then, looking at us with a smile, she used to say, "But first, let us pray the Rosary." So, there we were, all my friends and I praying the Rosary with my mom while the chocolate waited for us.

Everything in my childhood revolved around the Church and the faith. Mom used any situation as an opportunity to pray. When she cooked, she timed how long to boil eggs by praying Hail Marys. For soft-boiled eggs, you prayed twenty; if you wanted your eggs cooked more, you prayed longer. When I left the house, Mom would say, "Let's pray to your guardian angel." Then she would whisper, "Please, don't embarrass your guardian angel today." (I tried, but some days it was too difficult!) Mom always challenged us to be saints in our everyday activities. She often asked me and my sister what we were going to do that day to be holy. She didn't expect us to be perfect. Trying was enough.

My family wasn't unusual. This was the case for almost everyone I knew—my friends, my family, my community, and probably the whole country because our lives revolved around religious observances and festivities. This is why we could hardly wait for *las fiestas del pueblo* (the village festival) every year. It was a mix of secular and religious activity, but we all shared a very deep devotion to the patron of our town: Christ of the Consolation.

The stories of our patron date back to the Spanish Civil War when many churches were desecrated. If the people couldn't practice their faith openly, they did their best to protect what they could. One day, when a mob came to burn down the parish church, the sacristan removed the enormous and beloved crucifix. Unable to find a place big enough to hide it, he prayed to Christ, asking him to shrink the crucifix so he could hide it in a secure place. It seemed that the crucifix became smaller right in front of his eyes.

When the war was over, they looked for our crucifix with no success. Finally they looked under a stairway, knowing it would have been impossible to fit it in such a small space. But there it was! No one could believe how such a big cross would fit, and they had to break the wall to get it out. Of course, the crucifix was not only a reminder of the miracles of Christ, but a political statement. The enemy couldn't beat us completely in the war. We still had our big crucifix. We kept our faith. We won.

Years earlier a big drought had killed the farms and vine-yards, the main source of income. Our town needed a miracle, and there he was, our miraculous Christ. As it is custom in Spain, they processed through the streets of the entire town, with our Christ on the Cross, begging God to give them rain. It was May 17, 1925. As the procession was coming to an end, a torrent of water started pouring down on the happy villagers. It lasted three days and three nights.

Every year our town celebrates this miracle. Seventy years later, we still stop everything, and for three days, we eat and drink, we party, and we go to Mass. I am not sure if everyone is aware of the history behind the festivities. The devotion to our patron *el Cristo del Consuelo* (the Christ of the Consolation) is so great, though, that no matter what you really believe in or if you do not go to church the rest of the year, you celebrate with Christ and go to Mass with your family during the festival. For three days, we all feel a little better.

My village is not the only one with these types of stories. All towns in Spain have a patron with a miraculous story attached, and we all compete to see whose patron is the best or did the most powerful miracle. This may seem unusual to people living in other parts of the world, but it does bring communities together. Although deep faith might be lost over the years, the people still make God part of their lives, even if only because of tradition. Everyone wants to be married in the patron's chapel. Baptisms take place around the patron's cross as if the Christ of the Consolation is protecting the newborns. Confirmations and First Communions revolve around the patron's festivities. If you ask anybody around the village, we all have a common denominator: the Christ of the Consolation.

Our patron is a protector, an intercessor, a miracle worker—everyone in my town prays to our Christ when something goes wrong. You can see the holy cards placed near the beds of the sick, his image framed and hanging in every house, little statues on desks of desperate students who need to pass their college exams, stickers on car windows, and key chains, mugs, pens, and wallets with his design. And of course, Rosaries are said and hymns sung in his honor. It seems almost superstitious, as if we pray with a formula to a magician who is going to give us what we want. But deep inside, people still have a sense of the sacred: the love of a God who appears closer to us when we celebrate him this way.

We all go to God in desperate moments, and that is what happens in my town: war, hunger, death, desolation, and poverty bring us all together to God. At least once a year, we remember that we are human and not invincible. We remember that we need the protection and love of God. And we know that we need to pray because we are nothing without him.

But we can also forget. We can move on without taking all we are with us. That is what happened to me. Perhaps it has happened to you, too, or to someone you love. The strange thing is that even when we forget God, he doesn't forget us. Some part of the faith we once knew stays alive and hidden inside us. The devotion that remained in me even after I abandoned the Church was love for our Blessed Mother.

Ever since I can remember, I prayed the Rosary every day with my mom and my sister, and sometimes with my friends. Mom used to say that it was only ten minutes, but it was more like thirty after the addition of the Litany of Loreto and God-only-knows how many more Hail Marys for sinners, the poor souls in purgatory, and ten other causes. I honestly think we never stopped praying. Everything we did depended on a religious event, and there was always a certain prayer for every hour of the day. In the morning, we offered our day. At noon, we prayed the Angelus followed by the Rosary. At three, we prayed the Chaplet of Divine Mercy and some other novenas for saints and so on.

But as I grew older, I stopped praying the Rosary and the Chaplet of Divine Mercy. I stopped dressing up for Sundays or the day of my patron's festival. I hid all the emotions I had experienced praying in front of the Blessed Sacrament and how much fun I had singing for thousands of young people when I served as a music minister for religious congresses. I forgot who I really was for a while and lost most of what I had received from my family. But every night when I went to bed, maybe just as a routine or superstitious practice, I prayed a Hail Mary, just like Mom had always done with me. I don't remember what I prayed for. I don't know why I prayed. I just did.

Maybe you've held on to traditions that bring you warm memories without really knowing why. Or maybe you've left them behind because you were never very attached to them in the first place. Whatever the case, there was probably someone in your life who tried to give you what they thought was the most valuable thing they had: faith.

Sometimes, we aren't sure what to do with what we are given. It may not be what we hoped for or what we wanted. It may not "fit" or be "our style." We may leave it behind or throw it away or forget about it altogether. But faith never really disappears. One day, when I least expected it, my Catholic heritage stirred in me again. When I stepped into a church after many years, it all came back to me, and for the first time in a long time, I knew I was home. I knew in an instant who I really was, what I needed to do, and what I was called to be. But before that moment of grace, I traveled a different road, one that led me far away from the inheritance of faith and family I had been given.

Prayer of a Prodigal

Lord,
You know what a disaster I am.
I complain
And I demand everything from you.
I can be frustrated.
I can be lazy and impatient.
I am often in a hurry.
I didn't know how rich I was.
That's why it was easy to walk away,
To take what was coming to me and never look
    back.
I forgot you completely.
But now I remember
Because the things I thought I wanted aren't
    enough.
Please, Lord,
Give me the courage, the strength, and the wisdom
To seek you,
To find you,
To encounter you in everything I do,
To love you as I once did,
To love you as you always have loved me.
Amen.

3

A DISTANT COUNTRY

*A few days later the younger son gathered all he
had and traveled to a distant country, and there he
squandered his property in dissolute living.*
—*Luke 15:13*

In the environment I grew up in, it was only natural that I developed some type of religious vocation. Mom and Dad were not surprised when I wanted to follow Padre Pablo and become a priest. At the time, priests were respected and admired as the ones who brought us closer to God. Half our lives revolved around services that required a priest. When a priest walked through the town, everyone—Catholic or not—was nice to them. They were invited to have lunch here and dinner there. Women offered to clean their houses and cook for them. Padre Pablo was a celebrity, and being a priest was the "in thing." So, at the age of ten, I left home and went to a minor seminary in Toledo, Spain.

Most people think that an eleven-year-old could never make such an important decision. But back then, I didn't have to give up many things because I didn't really have many possessions. No large collections of electronics, clothes, or books.

In fact, my mom was strict about watching TV or playing outside for too long. Plus my intellectually disabled brother needed attention from all of us 24/7. Going to seminary was a kind of liberation. I met new people there and many are still friends to this day. We could watch TV and we had movie nights. There were game nights and sports during the day. I played anything and everything but loved the academics too. I worked hard because I always wanted to be the best at everything. I studied Latin and Greek, learned to play piano and guitar, and became interested in theater. I could never have done those things in my small town.

Seminary life both changed some of what I believed and also enriched the beliefs I brought with me. I started understanding the liturgy and the sacred spaces for prayer. Toledo is rich in churches, and the Gothic cathedral is the center of the city. Everything in the cathedral is so monumental and mysterious, but somehow, I felt at home. The lights made the liturgical places so pure and conducive to prayer. The carvings in the walls told all kinds of stories. The highly adorned altars drew me upward. The monstrance used for adoration seemed to me like a golden treasure. The songs, the long and thin columns, the smell of old stones, the silence, the transparent and biblical windows, all made it almost impossible not to pray. It really felt like the house of God.

But my favorites were the field trips and summer camps. Every summer, after spending a month at home for vacation, we students got together again in the middle of the mountains for a whole month living in pure nature. One of those years, I met a girl from a nearby camp and fell in love for the first time. This made me doubt my young vocation, and when the school year started, I wasn't motivated at all. The initial enthusiasm of the early years had become routine, and I started feeling trapped. I couldn't stop thinking about that girl even though she had forgotten about me. As a result, I began finding flaws in everything we did in seminary. I even got the nickname of "rebel with a cause." I tried to be expelled so I didn't have to make a decision to leave seminary and feel like a quitter. But in the end, that's exactly what I chose to do.

Going back to public school was so depressing. At seminary, I had been kind of a big thing. Everyone loved my bubbly, extroverted personality, and I was always the class rep, or the one in charge of things like the library, the chapel, or the rec hall. Now, in public school, I was a nobody. I spent all day with strangers and teachers who didn't even know my name. My grades dropped drastically, and all I could think of was going to weekend parties. After six months, I was failing all my subjects and asked my parents if I could quit school. I thought they would laugh at me, but my dad was dead serious when he told me, "Sure, you can quit. You don't have to go to school starting tomorrow." But at four o'clock the next morning, my dad woke me up to work with him in the vineyards.

After six very hard months, I decided to go back to school. This time I wanted to go big, so I applied to a school in Madrid. I started a degree in linguistics and dreamed of traveling the world. My heart was focused on living abroad and teaching in countries far away from home. I wanted to be wealthy and free from the limitations of poverty or living in a small town.

That's when my faith started to dissipate. I stopped going to Mass at home on the weekends and started lying to Mom about praying and going to Mass while I stayed in Madrid.

One Sunday without Mass became two Sundays, and then a month or two went by without Mass or even thinking about God. At first lying made me uncomfortable and disappointed with myself. But in time, it got easier. My college friends didn't go to church either, and Mom would never know.

My mom often told me that if I forgot to talk to God daily, then one day I would forget about him completely. She was right. The big moment came when I had the opportunity to travel and study abroad. Traveling to Berkeley and New York, studying and working a whole year in Washington, DC, my relationship with God was almost completely gone. I don't remember even thinking, "It is Sunday. I should at least pray." Being far from God became normal. In fact, I thought it was *necessary* if I wanted to achieve all I dreamed of. It never occurred to me that I could study, work hard, travel, and still be close to God. I chose the former.

Eventually a great opportunity came my way. I got a job in Wales. Finally I could be totally independent and guilt free. But earning money and living far away wasn't enough; I always wanted more. So, I applied to teach in the United States and got the job of my dreams at a high school in Los Angeles. My friends from college were so jealous. I was the one who had made it big. My friends from my small town treated me as if I was at the top of the pyramid, and I loved the feeling. I started making money and could buy all the things I could never get as a kid. I had some rich friends in Spain, but I was the one on top now. I invited those friends to visit me, paid for everything, and made sure I had more than they did. And it felt good.

I would have never thought that things like money and prestige would make me abandon God in such an extreme way. Yet, day by day, I stepped further and further from God. I lived as if I had never heard of God. I didn't even notice churches, Sundays, or big religious seasons like Lent. When I visited my parents, I could go to Mass with them as if nothing had changed, then fly back to my free, independent life in Los Angeles.

My issues were deeper than just wanting to own things or be successful in life. In time, I became like a robot who did things because that's the way life is supposed to be. So, I studied, worked hard, got a good job, made more money, and bought things. The more people admired my success and possessions, the more I wanted and the more I flaunted what I had acquired. That's how it works. Soon, unhappiness showed up, and the way to get rid of that feeling was more spending, more parties, more drinking, better social status, more showing off. Frivolous lifestyles are expensive. Eventually, they cost us everything.

We know that something is missing, but most of us never imagine that God could be part of the "solution." Instead we think that if we made it all the way to where we are, we can find our own way out. But that isn't what happens. God never leaves our side, and the minute we dare to utter his name, he comes to us, gently but with strength.

We might look back and feel sad about how easily and quickly we gave up on God. It all happens almost naturally, without effort. But when we know we're lost in a distant land far from home, we can turn around like the prodigal son and decide to return to the Father. I have tortured myself thinking that this was the wrong reason to make the journey home. I have wished that my reconversion came from more than mere sadness or encountering a roadblock in my life. But perhaps it was the only way to stop my fast pace in the wrong direction.

Whatever makes us turn around, we can thank God for it. No matter how much time we have wasted, no matter how low we have gone, God will make something beautiful of it all if we let him. He is always there and never uttering a "Well, well, well. Look who is back. Now that you need me, you decide to call my name." There is no land too distant, no pigsty too filthy for him. Sometimes the smallest thread of connection is enough to remind us that we are in a distant land, far from home.

Prayer of a Prodigal

When I am far from home,
When my dreams and expectations are lost,
When all I hoped for vanishes,
When I look for joy and peace and cannot find it,
When all I encounter is disappointment and dead
    ends,
When I want to have it all but I feel empty,
When I struggle for happiness but feel broken,
When I smile on the outside but know I am alone,
When this world takes everything I have away,
I want to turn to you, Lord,
Because I know in my heart
That you are
My joy
My peace
My hope
My love
My home
And my all.
Amen.

4

LOVE THAT WELCOMES

While he was still far off, his father saw him and
was filled with compassion; he ran and put his arms
around him and kissed him.
—Luke 15:20

On that April morning in 2005, I felt deep disappointment for my mother, for myself, and for God. Realizing that all my hope was gone, I started to cry like a little boy, alone and lost. I knew I needed to be saved, and I wanted to come back home, not just to the physical place I missed so much. I wanted to come back to my spiritual home. A place that was once very familiar and, even more, full of the happiness I so desperately desired.

The funeral of Pope John Paul II was still on the TV, but I couldn't concentrate anymore. And so, I began to pray. I had a deep urge to talk to God, to confess all my failures and tell him about my pain. I wanted to scream, but I couldn't. My throat was sore from crying, and at that moment, I suddenly realized something: I had forgotten how to pray, how to talk to God. I tried to remember the prayers Mom had taught me when I was a child, but for some reason, the Our Father didn't feel like enough. I had so much more to say, and "sorry" seemed like an easy way out of the guilt. So I continued to pray in silence, trying to breathe while gasping in tears. This was the only way I could communicate with God.

I was so deeply hopeless and hurt, so desperate to find a formula of words to say to God, but I couldn't muster anything. Then a terrifying thought struck me: What if my mother couldn't forgive me for all the years that I had lied to her about going to Mass on Sundays? Or about praying the Rosary? Every time I had visited my family in Spain, my mother would give me a bit of an interrogation. She was persistent, but because I loved her very much, I lied. "Of course I go to Mass, Mom." "Yes, yes. Every night before I go to bed, I pray three Hail Marys." But I hadn't gone to Mass for almost ten years, let alone made a Confession or prayed the Rosary.

I remembered coming back from partying one year and passing a Catholic church. People were coming out with candles and singing. It was either Holy Thursday or Good Friday. I smiled at the thought of how I had done the same when I was younger. At the time, I remembered attending spiritual retreats during Holy Week with the youth group and the priest in my town and actually having fun. But seeing those people singing and praying didn't change my heart. It just brought back a childhood memory, and I moved on.

I grew content with not wasting my time on Sundays with going to Mass, but instead sleeping in, watching TV all day, walking my dog, and going out to late parties with my friends. *I am a good person. I don't kill anyone. I don't need to go to church to be good.* There were a hundred thoughts

I used to justify myself. In fact, I was a good person. My friends thought of me as positive, caring, and generous. I was always there for them, paid for everything, and drove them everywhere for parties. I was always smiling and almost never argued with people. They all loved me. I didn't need my childhood god. Religion was something of the past, something for my mother, not me—not anymore.

But what was happening now? Why had all these feelings filled my heart again? And what was I supposed to do? I supposed I could ignore the whole experience and start drinking and partying again. After all, I had done that for ten years. I was an expert on fleeing painful situations and manipulating my mind into thinking that I was OK. I had learned to deal with unhappiness one day at a time. But I couldn't ignore all those "new" but familiar feelings anymore. Something had awakened in me, and it was unstoppable.

I knew had to tell my mother everything I had done. I didn't know what else to do or who else to call. If there was someone who "knew" things about God and how to talk to him, it was Mom. At least she would teach me how to pray again and I could learn how to say, "I am sorry," to God from my heart. I wasn't sure that my mother or God could ever forgive me. But as I sat there in my pigsty, drenched in sweat, tears, and fear, I realized that something had to change. I needed to change. I wanted to be better. I needed to be forgiven. And I desperately wanted another chance. I would have to start again, but I knew I couldn't do that alone. So, I stood up, picked up the phone, and called my mother.

Most of us don't even realize what real love is until we find ourselves surrounded by loneliness and rejection. Then pain becomes comfortable to the point that we accept that state of unhappiness. We feel sorry for ourselves because we think that nobody else cares for us. We feel abandoned and perhaps forgotten. And when we show others a moment of tremendous sadness, they feel so sorry for us, and that makes us feel wanted and momentarily loved. It is the trap of self-pity.

The answer we seem to forget is forgiveness. If we can't imagine forgiveness, we can't get out of the self-pity cycle. I feel sad and don't want to, but it feels good when others pay attention to me precisely *because* I feel sad. That is not love or forgiveness. It is a pride that feeds itself until the next time I need attention again. I know because I was caught in this cycle and full of this kind of pride.

Forgiveness, however, has the power to change our hearts. We just need the grace to forgive ourselves and the courage to ask for forgiveness. That's the first step toward a true and humble conversion. And it's not easy. That's why we need the power of God's love. I knew that I could forgive someone who was ten minutes late for dinner or never showed up for a movie date. In fact, I realized there were a number of things I could forgive—but betrayal wasn't one of them. I didn't understand the depth of forgiveness because I didn't understand the depth of love. As it turned out, God did forgive my betrayal of him. God didn't belittle me for returning to him as a broken person. No. Instead he opened his arms totally to me. And so did my mother.

The hardest thing for me was to admit that I had been wrong in so many things. It was going to be even harder to communicate this to my friends. I needed to find someone who would hear me out, not because of pity, but because of real love for me and the person I was becoming. Changing directions was going to be difficult, especially because the path feels lonely. But the truth is, we do not walk alone. God calls each one of us to return to him and provides the love and help we need for each step we take toward him. The question is, Are we ready to open our heart to God completely? Can we come to him with the guilt, the pain, and the shame and ask, "Do you still love me, Father? Can you forgive me?"

If you are making the journey to the Father's house, it's important to know that you will be welcomed home with love. What's even more amazing, though, is that there are other people like God himself, who see and love you even while you're still far away. I knew my mom would never say, "I told you so." She'd just love me and walk the first steps of the journey home with me.

So, I poured out my heart to Mom. It was a long and difficult conversation filled with silent, awkward moments. I told her everything I had done over the past ten years, wishing that she wouldn't ask many questions. I could hear some silent tears on the other end of the phone, and my voice quivered several times. "Mom, I am so sorry. I lied because I didn't want to hurt you," I ended up saying. "And now all I want to do is talk to God. Pray, I guess. But . . . but I don't remember how. I don't know what to say . . ." I closed my eyes tight, expecting to hear a reproach or maybe an exasperated sigh. Then Mom said, "OK. I will teach you how to pray the Rosary again, like when you were a little kid." And we prayed together.

Love is the response we are called to give one another, especially to those who have a longer journey to make. But sometimes we seem to care more about where someone has been than where they are headed. We become too comfortable and complacent where we are. We occupy ourselves so much with what's going on inside the Father's house that we don't even look down the road to see who might be coming, waiting to be welcomed with pure and unconditional love. If we do see someone who is lost, do we welcome them or do we judge a sinner for his sins instead? Do we try to use guilt or shame to reach someone? We must always remember the words of Jesus, "Just so, I tell you, there will be more joy in heaven over one sinner who repents than over ninety-nine righteous persons who need no repentance" (Lk 15:7). The journey home isn't made by sheer willpower, but by love—God's first and then ours.

Prayer of a Prodigal

Lord, I desire to come to you more than ever,
But I am scared and I feel alone.
I don't even know how to pray.
I don't even know where to start my journey,
But I want to trust in your love
And that you will send that person
Who will walk with me
Until I find myself in your arms again.
Amen.

5

INVISIBLE TRANSFORMATION

So he set off and went to his father.
—Luke 15:20

When I moved to the United States, all my intimacy with God and, in a way, all my Catholic heritage was moved to somewhere remote in my conscience. I thought I had forgotten everything, but my faith was still buried deep within me. While I remembered all the religious activities from my past, I was not living the same way as when I was a child, going to Mass with my parents, all dressed up, nice hair, all smiles, and a sense of "being good." All that seemed so far away.

But after talking to my mother, the cat was out of the bag, and I knew there was no way back to the way I had been living. This thought gave me peace and terrified me at the same time. For many days afterward, I almost regretted having taken this step. Some mornings I woke up with a happiness that filled my whole day and everything that happened to me. But other days I wished I could just go back to my pigsty and dismiss the hurricane of emotions that had changed my life.

I was afraid to start a new life. What was I going to tell my "secular" friends? No more parties because I had had a mystical experience? That I had encountered God and was now a religious fanatic? I knew they would laugh at me. I knew because over the previous ten years, my friends and I had laughed together at this kind of thing. Meeting those who had experienced God and changed their lives was like a clown show for us. My friends would probably think that someone had brainwashed me or that I had joined a cult.

So, I started to lie to my friends. Because I worked with many of them, it was difficult and mentally exhausting. The fake laughter and the disgusting jokes I pretended to embrace. The gossip and destructive comments about my boss and other coworkers. The uncharitable anger aimed at my students and the apathetic attitude about life. The ongoing parties with alcohol and drunkenness. The funny thing is that all of this had been me for the past ten years. It was all very familiar, but now it felt so painful. It made me sick both because my friends considered this behavior normal and also because I knew that that wasn't me anymore. Nevertheless, I couldn't stop it. Every day I woke up nervous and told myself, "Today is the day when I tell my friends. I can do it." But I couldn't, and one day became ten, and ten became three months. The worst part is that I was aware of everything so clearly and yet I didn't have the courage to tell them what had happened.

One late night, I took my dog for a walk. I was alone as I always was when I walked my dog this late, but that night I felt really alone. I was certain that nobody would ever understand what was in my heart. Heck, I didn't even understand what was happening to me. So, I made up my mind to live a double life. I could go to parties, drink, and gossip at night, and go to Mass and pray during the day. Suddenly I realized that I was just going from lying to my mother to lying to my friends. Right there, in the middle of that lonely, cold, dark night, I cried again.

I wasn't sad or happy, just alone, with no answers and no strength. When I got back home I was ready to give up. But I saw my old guitar in the closet. Without thinking, I pulled it out. There was a thick layer of dust, and as my fingers stroked the strings, it was as if I heard my guitar crying with me. My guitar was one of the few things from my past that accompanied me, waiting quietly in a case in the closet without reproach or condemnation. I tuned it, and my fingers took the position for the first chord. I felt the pain in my rusty fingertips. I had learned how to play when I was a youth minister in my little town. One time I played for hours and hours while we had a youth retreat, to the point that one of my fingertips started bleeding. It was a battle scar, and I felt almost proud and happy to have it.

My shaky right thumb made it all the way though the six strings, making a quiet sound from the guitar that had been silent for a decade. Music filled my room. My body shivered with goosebumps, but I couldn't stop now. I played and played all night long until I had the urge to sing something. I forgot I could pray like this. That night, I wrote a song called "Do Not Be Afraid." It was the beginning of telling my story in a different way. If my words couldn't find the strength to communicate what I felt, then I would sing it.

That invisible transformation changed me and gave me the strength to do something with what I was experiencing. I needed to practice, to make some effort to start my new journey. I couldn't just put my new life in a case and hide it in a closet to accumulate dust. Sooner or later, I would have to take my problems out of the case and set off for the Father's house. The longer I waited, the more my fingers—and all of me—would hurt.

———

It is interesting that in seeking power, happiness, and purpose, we run fast from the One who can give us real freedom, joy, and hope. Instead we create our comfortable spaces and build the four walls that can allow us just enough light to survive. Then God destroys those four walls and shows us the sun, the real light. When our walls are destroyed, we can feel like part of us is dying. Mourning the loss of my "hard working" years of living in the world, suddenly, I saw the bigger illumination again. It was at that moment that I realized I had just begun to walk in the right direction.

When we feel the sun once more, we instinctively return to what we know, or once knew in our childhood traditions. I had an urge to go to Mass every day, and so I did. It was very strange to be in a place so familiar, yet one I had chosen to forget. Guilt came again. That's often what happens if we lose a treasure and someone returns it, even though we never bothered to search for it. We feel like failures.

Happiness and regret make a strange mix. It is like putting alcohol in an open wound: it hurts, but it's a good and healing pain. I had the urge to spend hours in a chapel and just sit there. Every time I went to Mass or spent hours in the chapel, all I did was cry. Guilt, sorrow, shame, and self-condemnation were the first feelings, but they quickly disappeared. I still cried, but I wasn't sure whether I was happy or sad. I just cried. As I felt God's love for me, I remembered how much I had once loved God. I returned to my memories, looked up all my friends from seminary and all the priests who had helped me along the way. I researched novenas, how to pray the Rosary, spiritual books, and different religious communities. I fell in love with God and my tradition, but this time it was chosen freely and as an adult.

The prophet Jeremiah said, "O LORD, you have enticed me, and I was enticed; you have overpowered me, and you have prevailed" (Jer 20:7). In Spanish, it translates as, "You seduced me, Lord, and I let myself be seduced." This verse is meaningful to me because the first time I opened my Bible after it spent many years collecting dust, that was the verse I read. And this is what that moment of sweet confusion feels like. Deep inside, we know that it is a healing pain. Even though it exposes our humanity and makes us vulnerable, it opens our hearts not only to God, but also to ourselves. And that is just the beginning of a new future in love with God.

If you are at this moment in your life, go gently. It is likely that you will encounter many obstacles and much pain as you try to understand what to do and how to do it. Be patient. Things don't change overnight. It takes a lot of talking to God—peaceful days but also painful ones. You may wonder whether maybe you made a mistake. After all, how can something as incredible as encountering God after many years be so difficult?

Looking back, I am glad it wasn't easy. If it had been, I wouldn't have put so much of myself into it. It would have been a simple chore with a check mark next to it. But setting off for the Father is much more than that. It is a way to live.

Don't be afraid of the difficulties that getting closer to God might bring. Embrace them, surrender, pray, and stand up. From here on, you'll need to keep taking one step after the other.

Prayer of a Prodigal

Lord,
Give me the strength to take the next step,
To follow the way that leads to you
In my daily circumstances.
Even when things don't go the way I want,
Even when I don't know how to talk to you,
Even when I don't feel you,
Even when I am convinced you are not there,
And especially when I am about to give up.
With your strength, I know I can
Find my way to you.
And loving you,
I can hope and trust
That you will always heal
What is so broken in me.
Amen.

6

GROWING PAINS

"I have sinned against heaven and before you."
—Luke 15:21

The journey back to God is rarely steady or straight. I had days when all I could think was to pray and spend time with God in the chapel, and other nights when I went back to drinking and partying with friends. Of course, that was accompanied with regret and guilt the next day, as well as a strange feeling of failure. But the inability to forgive myself was something I couldn't get over.

I wanted to tell my mother about this roadblock, but I was too ashamed of myself for not following through on my new love for God and the change I desired. Discouraged, I started to go back to my old ways more often. I was convinced that my mother wouldn't forgive my "relapses." That was my constant daily thought, so I gave up. Again.

I finally opened up about my situation to a friend, a classmate in seminary who was now a priest. He was a bit surprised to hear my voice after so many years, but even more shocked when he heard my story. I noticed that it was easier for me to retell my past ten years to him than it had been with my mother. Yet my friend's many moments of silence made me really uncomfortable. I think I could even hear his mind judging me and my life. But after a while, he suggested something to me. "I think you need to go to Confession." Now I was the one being silent.

Confession? Was he crazy? It's one thing to try to be better, a new person, even opening up to people little by little, struggling to deal with my friends. But now I had to shock a priest with all my sins? I didn't think so. Too soon. Too difficult. I didn't even know of any Confession times at the Catholic churches around me. When I found a church and a priest for Confession, what would I do? Would I just go in and scream, "Any priest here brave enough to hear my sins?" Now I imagined my friend smiling at me in my silence, so I asked him whether we could just do it over the phone and get it over with. Then he really chuckled out loud. "No, no, no," he said. "That's something you have to do in person. Don't you have several Catholic churches around you?" "I don't know. I guess I can find one." Now I had to deal with yet another obstacle.

I was embarrassed because I had forgotten how to go to Confession. I knew there were things I was supposed to say before and after, but I didn't remember any of them. I think my friend could sense my stress, so he offered to walk me through the whole thing. "I call Confession the sacrament of anxiety," he said, "so I understand what you are feeling. I feel it too. Imagine a priest, who is supposed to be good, going to Confession!" Then he told me what to do. I took notes of everything almost as if I was preparing for an exam. At the end of our conversation, he wished me good luck and said he would pray for me. Then he thanked me for sharing with him such a precious private moment.

Some days later as I was driving by a Catholic church, I decided to rip off the bandage and just do it. As I entered the church looking for a priest, I realized I didn't have my notes with all the prayers I needed or my long list of sins. As I was leaving, an older-looking priest greeted me and asked if he could help me, so I just shouted out, "Yes. I want to make a Confession." I couldn't feel my legs, but like a zombie, I followed the priest. It was dark and I could hear the echo of our steps, louder and louder, along with the pounding beat of my heart. I sat down in a very dark "box," and there was a very long and uncomfortable silence.

The prayers I rehearsed over and over were gone. *What do I do? What do I say? How do I start? How do I get out of here?* I was sweating and felt totally paralyzed. Just when I was about to say something, the priest asked, "When was the last time you went to Confession?" "Ten years," I said. Then with a kind smile, he asked if I needed help. I almost cried of joy. "Yes, please. I am very nervous. I forgot how to do Confession." "It is OK," he said. "I am glad you are nervous. You are about to do the most important thing: ask for forgiveness. It can't be easy, but it has great value." As he guided me through the process, he explained to me what I could do the next time. He suggested writing my sins down on a piece of paper so I wouldn't be too nervous trying to remember them. And at the end he said, "Don't be afraid. I will pray for you."

I left the confessional, and as I kneeled to pray my penance, I started to weep. I don't know whether it was the release of stress or that I was overwhelmed with peace. But at the time, I didn't care if my sobbing filled the whole church, because I felt not only forgiven, but a tremendous joy that no one had judged me, or made fun of me, or even yelled at me. Instead he had listened with a tender smile.

I stayed there in the dark, silent church for over an hour. I wanted to scream, "Thank you!" to God, but silence and tears were my only prayers of thanks. I didn't remember feeling this overwhelmed when I went to Confession in my youth. But after so many years of carrying my sins with me, the joy of feeling free was too powerful for me to even try to speak. It was a major jump in my journey.

———

I still remember that moment whenever I return to the Sacrament of Penance (Confession) today, especially now as a priest. Don't get me wrong. I still get nervous when I go to Confession, and I think I will always get this kind of anxiety. But that's OK because, as that priest said, I am about to do something important, something that requires more than just waiting in line to order coffee. God's forgiveness is extraordinary, and it requires an extraordinary decision and some preparation.

Now as a priest, I encounter many people approaching the confessional with the same anxiety I had. It's OK to feel anxious. But it's also important to remember that you are about to do something extraordinary. Asking God to forgive you will change your life. So, being nervous is just part of doing something great.

When I see joy, peace, and relief in people's faces, it reminds me of the loving Father welcoming his prodigal son. The son walked that journey with much anxiety, sadness, and guilt, but he found strength to repent and walked all the way home. He expected rejection, anger, judgment, and shame, but instead he got forgiveness, love, and the embrace of the father who was always waiting for him with open arms.

I don't know what you feel about Confession. Whatever you feel, don't be afraid of the obstacles you encounter, that priest who treated you unkindly, or your personal fears. All it takes for us to receive God's mercy is knowing how much we need it. The words "I have sinned" are powerful because they are true for all of us. But remember that there is no sin too big for God to forgive. He loves us that much and more. When you take this step forward to the Father, you will find that he has already taken many steps toward you.

Prayer of a Prodigal

Lord,
I come before you
With a broken heart,
Knowing that I don't deserve you,
But I need you.
Here I am, Lord, hoping that
Beyond my sins, there is your forgiveness.
Beyond my brokenness, your love.
Beyond my regrets, your consolation.
Beyond my loneliness, your presence.
Beyond my sadness, the joy of being loved by you.
Here I am, Lord.
This is all I have.
Here I am, Lord.
This is my wounded and open heart.
Amen.

7

ON SPEAKING TERMS

I will get up and go to my father, and I will say
to him . . .
—Luke 15:18

In every relationship, we bring our baggage with us, and so I did with God. The only difference was that he already knew about me, about my guilt, my sin, my lying life, my darkness, and my unforgiving attitude. Still, he wanted to love and forgive me. I wasn't ready for this, because I didn't love myself much, let alone forgive myself. But the moment I started opening up to God, I felt so much love and so little judgment. It was as if he had been waiting for this moment, knowingly preparing me to return home. God met me in the pigsty where I was. As I tried to bring my past to him, I knew I could not hide anything from him. But that didn't keep me from wanting to pray.

The process was very ordinary. It was just me, nothing to hide, nothing to prove, no need to impress. It was just me with a naked soul and a wounded heart. And there, in that intimacy, in the peaceful stage of my life, I fell in love with God again. Wounds started to heal, trust flowed effortlessly, and I felt the love of God, just like when I was a child. Now I wanted to love him back, and I wasn't sure how or where to start. Prayer seemed the logical thing to do.

I thought prayer wasn't going to be that easy, because I had so many feelings that I couldn't share with any of my friends, let alone explain those feelings to another person, so all I could do was talk to God. I had been used to reciting prayers that someone else wrote, praying the Rosary, or just saying multiple Our Fathers and Hail Marys. I remembered my mom had many prayer books. I knew the basic forms of prayers and that they all ended in "Amen." I was sure that just talking to God was not enough, or even considered a prayer, but I just couldn't stop it. I talked to him on my way to work, when walking my dog, at home, and at the gym. But I still felt as if something was missing, so I decided to find a chapel.

I started going to Mass every day, but I wanted to find a quiet chapel, without many people, where I could be alone with God. A place where I didn't need to explain all these feelings to God, because he already knew everything about them. I remember asking people at Mass if they knew a place where I could pray late after work. They all looked at me like I was out of my mind. "Here at the church," an annoyed lady once told me. "You are here now. Why can't you pray *here?*"

She wasn't wrong, but for some reason I just couldn't concentrate after Mass. Too many people around me. Too much noise. Too many distractions. I just wanted to be alone, and I didn't really know why. I felt as if I wouldn't have enough time to be with God in the short time before they closed the church after Mass. I wanted God all for myself for as long as I needed. It was a strange feeling, but it was also hard to shake off.

Every day I hoped to discover a quiet chapel, and every day I was fairly sure that God would soon send me to a place where he could really hear me pray. Nobody had smartphones to search the internet at the time. So, I was on my own, driving around the city from church to church, looking for a place to pray.

One day I left work later than usual, so I knew I had to hurry if I was to be on time for the beginning of Mass. I drove the same way as always, but traffic was heavy. At that speed I would have never made it to Mass, so I decided to exit the freeway to an unfamiliar street and see if I could make up some time. The route wasn't much faster, and I knew I was going to be late for Mass. As I stopped at a traffic light, I started asking God for a traffic miracle, and as I turned my head to the right, my jaw dropped. Right in front of me, as I was stuck in traffic, stopped at this never-ending red light, I saw the answer to my prayers.

The sign said "Pauline Books and Media." I recognized the words. It was a Catholic store. When I was a child, I used to go to Madrid with my parents to a store with the same sign. They had so many books and music, medals of saints, rosaries, and all kinds of Catholic stuff. I remembered going there with my youth group and the priest from our small town. We spent hours and hours checking out all the amazing things they had. I couldn't believe there was one of those stores here too. I pulled into that small parking lot and took a breath. I was getting excited just thinking of all the things I wanted to buy. Maybe some prayer books, or books on the lives of the saints, or a special book that would help me.

As I entered, a small Filipino sister wearing a blue habit greeted me as if she had been waiting for me all day. "Hi,

I'm Sr. Joseph. I am happy to see a young man coming to our store today. Have you thought of becoming a priest?" I couldn't believe how peaceful and yet forceful that nun was! I didn't know what to say, but I smiled and I uttered something like, "A priest? I don't think I can be a priest. I don't even belong to a church!" I joked. "Oh, that's no problem. We can fix that." And taking my hand, she started walking me through the store. I wasn't sure what was happening or where she was taking me, but my head was spinning looking at all the books and other religious items. All of a sudden, we stopped in a doorway near the back of the store and she said, "Before you shop you must visit our chapel and say hello to Jesus."

A *chapel*? Did she just say a chapel? Did I hear her right? The chapel I have been praying for all this time? I couldn't believe that this store had a chapel and it had been there all this time for me to use. I felt overwhelmed, paralyzed, and full of adrenaline at the same time. I stared at that door for some time, and as I was about to enter, Sr. Joseph said, "If you need prayer books, we have some inside. Now go and pray. We close in three hours."

I will never forget the moment I entered that small, carpeted chapel. It was like going into another world. I was sure God had answered my prayers, but I wasn't sure how this had happened! I looked around and I found a chair in the rear of the chapel leaning against a wall. I knew that was the best place for me to pray. I didn't dare to be *too* close to God. I sat down and noticed another person sitting right up front. After ten minutes, she stood up. As she was about to leave, she genuflected and smiled at me before exiting. And then,

I was finally alone with God. It was at that moment that I knew I had arrived at home.

It still amazes me how God meets us where we are with a powerful yet gentle push. He pushed me hard enough to wake me up, but not to knock me on the floor. And so the romance began. I wanted to know more about God. I had been there before. I had prayed with my mother every day and belonged to a youth group that I used to lead in prayer. For some reason, all those times seemed like just something in the past, not connected to how I was feeling now. Perhaps I had just done what I was "supposed to do" in my relationship with God, but not with the desire of making it a two-way street.

This time I wanted to be part of this relationship. I wanted to know the one who was loving me and I wanted to know why. I spent hours and hours in silence. No questions, no answers, no feelings. Just us. I felt comfortable there, in that place where nobody could tell me that I didn't deserve anybody's love. Just the opposite, I felt as if a clean slate was presented before me with no regrets and nothing asked in return. Just us.

I think we often approach prayer as if it is a time when "we make" God present to us as if we "invoke" his presence by praying. In reality, God is always present and, when we pray, we make ourselves truly present to him. After I went to Confession, all I desired was to be with God. All those years I had been running away from him. The moment I was forgiven, I turned around to find that God was right beside me, waiting for me.

A lot of people find prayer difficult, not because the words of a written prayer are difficult to pronounce or because praying requires a special skill. Prayer is difficult because it requires being present to God as he is always present to us. Prayer requires us to be vulnerable before God and to show him all we have. Words are easy to say, and they help us with prayer many times. But what God really wants is our hearts, and that we open them completely to him. That's the part that is more difficult to achieve. The first step is showing up once we have the desire to talk with him.

Don't be discouraged if you think you don't know what to say, because silence in the presence of God is also a natural way to pray. There have been many times in my life when I have been with friends who are experiencing tough situations. They didn't demand that I speak all the time. They just wanted me to be there with them. God wants the same from us. He wants us to be there with him.

Many have asked me what's the best prayer they can pray, and I always tell them that the best prayer is for them to be with God. Then words will come or not. Be there first. I pray in many different ways. Sometimes it is the Rosary, some other times just Our Fathers, but many times I just say words and let God form the sentences because he knows me well and knows what is in my heart.

Don't approach prayer as a chore to get done but as a way of living your days in the presence of God. Even the greatest saints knew that we can pray even when we are doing other things (like cooking, driving, or walking the dog). We can also pray simply by being alone in a quiet, small chapel somewhere. Prayer will not change God's opinion of us, but it will change how we love him and one another.

Prayer of a Prodigal

Father, here I am.
Sometimes I don't even know how to pray,
And I hope that my deepest desire to talk to you
Is already the beginning of my prayer.
Father, here I am.
I give you everything:
My love,
My hopes,
My sins,
My pains,
My frustrations,
My silence,
And my desire
To love you more.
Father, here I am.
I am yours.
Amen.

8

FROM CONSOLATION TO DESOLATION

I am no longer worthy to be called your son.
—Luke 15:19

Since I discovered the bookstore chapel, I was hooked. I kept the image of the chair against the back wall in mind throughout each day, waiting for the time I would be sitting in it in God's presence. Every morning I woke up with that moment in mind and, after work, I got in my car and drove there in excitement. If there was a delay in traffic, I became impatient and a bit upset that I was wasting time that I could have been enjoying with God.

My routine became very noticeable for the nuns at the store and the regular customers who started getting to know me, or at least the *new* me. I liked the "me" they got to know: the good guy who came to pray every day at the same time. Yet my past was still too present in me. It was something that I wasn't going to disclose to anyone, especially to the holy nuns at the bookstore. Guilt and the fear of being judged prevented me from being too honest.

The only place where I was completely myself was in that chapel, so naturally I wanted to get there as soon as possible. It didn't matter what I was going to pray or say to God as long as I was with him. Many days all I wanted to do there was cry. I wasn't sure why, but I felt so much love there that tears were my natural response. Other days peace was my companion, and I could sit for three hours in complete silence. I loved those feelings so much that I became dependent on them. Whether I cried or I felt at peace, it was all the same to me: they were good feelings that kept me coming back to spend more time with God.

One day, as I headed back to the chapel, my eyes caught a glimpse of a book on prayer titled *Praying in Moments of Desolation*. I didn't know what desolation was, but if it was a book on prayer, I was interested. So after my three hours in the chapel, I bought that book on my way out.

One of the sisters whom I had formed a friendship with told me that it was a deep book on prayer. She pointed out the importance of acknowledging the moments of desolation in our lives. I was worried that she would think I was not a good Catholic (or not very smart) if I did not know what desolation was, so I just agreed with her. I counted on finding out the meaning of desolation when I read the book. I was very excited to go home and get started.

I finished the book that night, but I still didn't know what desolation was. The author described ways to pray daily, whether at work or driving, when at Mass or shopping. Pray always, no matter what. I was kind of happy to find out that I was doing that already. I mean, I was at the chapel for three hours on most days. How much more could I pray?

Some weeks later, as I went into my chapel expecting my prayer routine, things started feeling a bit dry. I felt something I hadn't felt before: I just didn't want to be there. There was some kind of impatience screaming in my brain, "Get out. Go home. Rest. Do something else." I lost the peace and deep emotional love I had experienced there from the beginning. For the first time, I wanted to leave. I couldn't understand why. It was as if I felt . . . nothing.

I wasn't used to that, at least not in the chapel. There were always these exuberant waves of emotions that made it easy to talk to God. Time usually went by fast because I felt so good in those three hours. I had so many things to tell him and to thank him for. Even in silence I felt inundated with feelings, and many days I just spent time repeating the words "thank you" over and over. It was always more than enough. And then *nothing*?

So, I did something I had not done since the first day I stepped in that chapel: I left after fifteen minutes of "prayer." I didn't know what to do. Could my prayer have run its course? Was there such a thing as a limit on prayer life, and after that, well, you are done? I went into the store and grabbed some books on spirituality and tried to browse through them on the sofa in the reading area, but I wasn't really interested. My mind was still a bit bothered about feeling nothing in the chapel, so I decided to return there and give it another try. Maybe I was doing something wrong? Or God decided to turn his back on me? I wouldn't blame him. It would have been really difficult to forgive me. Maybe God was finally showing me how mad at me he was for all of my sins.

Back on my chair in the chapel, I concentrated really hard and started to look for those feelings of wonder and love, joy and tears, the butterflies in my stomach and peace. I tried to feel something. But it was worse than nothing. Even feeling nothing would have been *something*. It would have given me a place to start a conversation, but this was worse. My mind felt empty. A complete void. So, I went home.

On my way home I did feel something: guilt and disgust. How could I have run out of prayer? What did I do wrong for God not to show up? Why did I quit so fast? Part of me wanted to go back to the chapel for yet another try, and a stronger part of me just didn't feel like it. I was worried this would be my new routine: show up to the chapel, say, "Hello, God," and leave. I didn't want that. I wanted to feel full of emotions so I could pray again.

The next day, I decided I would ask somebody who knew more about prayer than I did about what might be going on. When I entered the store, I was glad to see Sr. Frances, who was always very nice to me. We had shared spiritual conversations before. I usually just said hello and then went to the chapel, but I lingered a bit longer at the counter this time. After a while, she asked, "What, no praying today?" I was so glad she asked, and just like that, I started telling her how my prayer had been so amazing for some months now and how I felt full of love every time I entered the chapel; my tears of joy, repentance, and thanksgiving were always there. The three hours I stayed there felt like five minutes. But all of a sudden, I told her, I just didn't feel anything and I didn't even want to be there.

Sr. Frances listened to me quietly, smiling from time to time. I finally stopped talking, mainly because I wanted some answers from her. She motioned me toward the reading area so we could finish the conversation in private. "What you are experiencing is desolation," she said.

Desolation? Is that what this was? "Desolation is so important in the life of the prayer," Sr. Frances went on. "Desolation is when you don't feel anything, as opposed to consolation when you felt all those amazing emotions." I felt both relieved and a bit confused but interested in learning more. "Desolation is important because we must pray in all situations, not only when we feel something."

Sr. Frances also shared an example of what she meant by desolation: "It is like when you go out with your friends and have a good time. But other times you go out with your friends and maybe you are just bored. Regardless, you were with your friends, and you don't stop being friends because you had a boring day out. Prayer is something like that. Even when you don't feel anything, stay there. Love God. Give him your boredom and your lack of feelings, because he is always there. Your feelings have nothing to do with his presence and his love for you."

That day my prayer life changed forever. It became not just about me and what I felt, but a relationship with God—a relationship that started with me showing up whether I felt like it or not.

The truth is that prayer is very easy. It is as easy as showing up, or reading words from a prayer book, or just reciting the Rosary or making a novena. The enemy of prayer is not prayer itself but our own feelings. Most people who have tried to pray will eventually feel nothing, just as I did. They will also feel like giving up and running away. They will believe that God is absent or, even worse, has abandoned them.

In those situations, we may conclude that God is not listening and he, therefore, won't answer our prayers. I have been there so many times. What is really happening is that we allow our own feelings to highjack our time with God. Prayer is not a magic formula or a bribe for God to do what I ask of him. Prayer is much more than that. It is a moment we spend with the One who loves us more than we love ourselves. It is time for telling him everything or just nothing. Prayer is transforming because, in fact, we are never alone. God is always with us and never leaves our sides.

If you are walking this journey with someone who is experiencing the moments of desolation or consolation in prayer, remind them of the reality of prayer. Sometimes there will be joy and strong emotions, and other times just silence and nothing else, but we still show up.

One of the things I did during this time of learning about my prayer life was to keep one diary of my moments of consolation and another with my times of desolation. Whenever I felt nothing and I wanted to abandon my prayer, I read my consolation moments diary, and it was a reminder for me that *feelings* were just a small part of prayer. When I was in consolation mode, when I felt like angels were singing to me, I read my desolation diary. It helped me realize that emotions were just that—feelings, but not the substance of my prayer.

When helping someone in prayer, don't just pray *for* them; pray *with* them. Show them all those moments that accompany prayer, and help them discover the beauty that comes from being with God regardless of how we feel. Then prayer becomes the experience of the presence of God in everything we do, however we feel, and in both suffering and joy. In moments of desperation and moments of complete ecstasies we can live every day as if it were a prayer. Because it can be.

Prayer of a Prodigal

Lord,
I come to you with
My failings,
My disappointments,
My weaknesses,
My regrets,
My emptiness,
And my sins.
I know that I am not worthy of
Your forgiveness,
Your consolation,
Your strength,
And your love.
But here I am,
At your feet,
Asking for your presence
And your love
So I can start
To love you again.
Amen.

9

A DAILY YES

He was lost and is found.
—Luke 15:24

Prayer is very important, but it is not a magical formula that changes us overnight or grants our wishes as if we were dealing with a genie. St. Teresa of Calcutta once said, "I used to believe that prayer changes things, but now I know that prayer changes us and we change things." My journey toward the Father was not something that happened instantly. I moved slowly and changed little by little.

My new life had just begun, and even though I was full of emotions and a bit overwhelmed by it all, I understood this was going to be a day-to-day journey. I had to learn how to adjust to normal situations and face them in new ways. The first challenge came with the worldly friends with whom I had spent much time going out to parties and doing nothing related to church. It was easy during the week when I was alone. I could just drive to Mass and the chapel to pray in the middle of the afternoon. I knew I wouldn't see any of my friends in those places.

At first I was happy to be alone with God and didn't feel like I was lying to my friends, since they never asked me what I did on my own time after work. They probably assumed I was following my routines: Driving home. Taking a nap. Walking my dog. Going to the gym. I was content with them not knowing about my prayer life and interest in God. But after a while, a bit of a guilty conscience started to settle in.

Was I lying to my friends? Would they mock me for my newfound religious attitude? I thought they would laugh. I had laughed with them in the past. I remembered driving by a church with them and seeing a lot of people coming out of it. It must have been a Sunday. We all started mocking those people and laughing at how they had been brainwashed by priests and the Church just to con them out of their money. Whether I believed that or not, I was part of it. I was sure they would call me a hypocrite. "A hypocrite with a well-deserved adjective placed before it," I thought many times.

Was I a hypocrite? I thought about my fear of telling them about my new ways. I mean if I was really "reconverted" and I believed my faith to be true, then why was I such a coward about my love for God? Obviously, I wasn't as good as I thought, or I would be full of zeal, proclaiming all the things God had done for me. It would have been an incredible witness to my friends. But I just couldn't do it. Not yet.

My friends at work were another problem. After work, we used to go to happy hours together. There was nothing wrong with that, but for me, it was less time with God, so I started lying. "Not today. I am tired." "I can't today. I have a doctor's appointment." "I promised my neighbor I would walk her dog." "I have to take my dog to the vet." I wondered how long I could keep it up. Every time I went to Confession, the priest encouraged me to take the next step and tell my friends, but I failed every time.

I did pray for my friends to understand and love me, the new me. I prayed that they would also love God the same way I was learning to do. But after a while, I changed my prayer. I needed courage to be the new me when I was with them. Time went by, and something almost miraculous happened. They started to notice a difference in me. I thought I was the same person I had been, but I wasn't. My attitude and demeanor were different. "You are more peaceful," they began to tell me. Or, "You seem less stressed."

I started to sense that they were guessing something was up. I had spent a lot of time with them, and many days, we recapped our wild weekends while in the teacher's lunch-room. We also gossiped about our coworkers and our principal. Then I stopped participating in those conversations. I stopped gossiping. I quit swearing too. I just didn't feel comfortable with any of that kind of talk anymore. I wanted to be good and loving, so I decided to eat my lunch alone. I would even go to my car and pray a decade of the Rosary.

Eventually, I noticed the change in me too. I felt more joyful, content, and patient. I began to pray for my students on the way to work, and that helped me to be less irritated with them. My coworkers saw all of this, and to my surprise, they liked it. After a few weeks, they came to my classroom one by one to have lunch with me. They understood that my classroom was a gossip- and cursing-free space! And I felt like I was telling them about my faith without using words. For me, this was a comfortable way to communicate my love for God without having to use words.

One day, my friends and I were making plans for a Sunday brunch as we used to do. We were going to meet up at noon in our favorite restaurant, but as much as I wanted to go, I told them I couldn't, because I was going to Mass at noon. The conversation stopped, and we had what I thought was a very uncomfortable silence, until my best friend said, "Mass as in a Catholic Mass?" "Yes," I said. Trying to be very strong and convinced of my answer. "Then let's meet after. Would that work?" We all agreed, and I felt as if I had just won the biggest victory of my life. I drove home that day with such joy and peace.

It turned out to be only a small victory. I realized that every single day I had to say yes to God. Yes to really loving him, but even more so to really meaning it and acting like it. Sometimes I went back to my former ways, even missing Sunday Mass here and there, partying, drinking, and swearing more than I'd like to admit. But every new day, I had the choice of saying yes once again. The saddest part was that my inconsistency made my friends doubt my commitment to practicing my faith. I was disappointed that I was not being a good example to them.

I realized then that I couldn't do this alone. I started talking to my nun friend at the bookstore and the priest confessor, who each listened to me without judgment. I stopped hiding who I was becoming. My secular friends knew of my religious life, and my church friends knew of my former life. God knew it all, of course, and was there from the beginning to the end of each day. His constant forgiveness in Confession and his open arms every time I returned from one of my falls gave me the strength to continue saying yes to him with all my strength. I was far from perfect, but I opened up my wounds so I could heal and learn from my mistakes. I was full of scars from the moments when I fell, stood up, fell once more, and then was picked up yet again by God. God's love of me in these moments made me love him even more.

My friends ended up realizing that I had changed and, for the most part, they accepted it. It took a while for them to believe that I was now a "religious person" who had discovered God. That was the best way they could explain it. They watched me return to God time after time. They didn't convert, become religious, or start going to Mass. But they understood that the love of God had really changed me. And it was all God's doing.

I don't know if you have passed through this part of your journey, the part where you leave your old self behind. I know this is a painful process because you have to deal with the guilt of your previous life and leaving some old friends behind. But once you have experienced the Father who welcomes you with open arms, unconditionally and with complete love, there is no reason to fall back to your previous ways.

Don't be afraid of your falls and failures, because it is not just you walking this path. God has you in his arms and he won't let go. Say yes to him every day. Don't worry about what you have to say to others about your new life. It is your actions that will tell your friends and the world that you are loved, forgiven, and lifted up. Continue to show up, spend time with God, and be transformed. Tell him your fears, your failures, your joys, and your victories, and let him accompany you. The journey is your journey to make, but you do not make it alone.

Maybe you know someone who is struggling in this process of getting to know God. Or maybe someone you know is struggling to confront their fears that friends and maybe even family won't accept their encounter with God. Talk to that person. Let them know that you are there with them, with no judgment. Let them know you will listen to their frustrations, confusions, and fears. Let them know they are not alone. Wherever you are in your own journey, you can help bridge a person's old life with their new life in Christ.

Finally it is important to know that you don't have to break with your old world completely when you meet God. You can hang out with your friends. You can have a good time. Just remember that you belong to God, and he wants you to show others that you are his. When you spend time together, witness to your faith by your actions, first of all, and your words too. My mother used to say that love will change the world, but we have to be in the world in order to show it love. Don't be afraid of the obstacles on this journey; rather, bring your love for God to everything and everyone. And watch it change the world.

Prayer of a Prodigal

I thank you, Lord,
Because I left you,
But you didn't give up on me.
I rejected you,
But you didn't give up on me.
I offended you,
But you didn't give up on me.
I was lost,
And you came to find me,
Because you never give up on me.
Amen.

10

A GOD OF TEARS

"He ran and put his arms around him and
kissed him."
—Luke 15:20

My deepest moments of consolation happened during Mass, but appreciating Mass was not easy for me at first. For as long as I can remember, I had gone to Mass with my parents, not only on Sundays but many times during the week. I was familiar with all of the liturgical rituals, but for some reason, Mass seemed foreign and new to me on my return.

I remember feeling embarrassed to ask my mom to help me with the responses for Mass. I thought she would yell at me. I had been a church person almost all my life; how was it possible that after only ten years I had forgotten how to pray at Mass? But very calmly and patiently, we rehearsed. After a few phone calls with my mom, I had thought Mass would feel as if I hadn't missed a decade of Sundays. That was not really the case.

After checking schedules for daily Masses in several churches, I found one I could go to in the evening. It was a nice church. Very quiet and not many people. I sat in the back, far enough away from everyone so they didn't think I was ignorant if I didn't know all the prayer responses, but also close enough to hear them and observe their movements.

It was at the first Mass I attended after being absent for so many years that I experienced my first big moment of consolation. The priest came out of the sacristy to preach his homily, some people in the front started to sing, and out of nowhere, I began to cry. I wasn't sad or happy, just literally moved to tears. I couldn't stop crying the whole Mass. A couple of people looked back to see what was happening, but it didn't bother me. I just kept on crying. It was such an awakening. As if time had been still since I was a child. My memories of when I was child were totally alive, but this time I felt as if God had put his arms around me.

My life flashed before me, the good and the bad. I felt loved and unworthy all at once. I felt as if God saw me, as I am, with all my wounds, past sins, and scars. I could see the Father with open arms, waiting for my return, and all I could answer was with my tears. Everything was alive for me, as if my senses were totally functioning at high speed. I was so aware of every answer, prayer, and movement of the priest around the altar. It felt like I had truly arrived at home.

When Mass ended, I was emotionally exhausted and overwhelmed but full of joy. I just sat there in my pew, trying to absorb every moment. It felt like I was in heaven, or at least in the most peaceful place on earth. I was so happy I had decided to come to Mass, despite the anxiety it initially caused me. I couldn't wait to come back the next day, and the next, and always. Such was my consolation that day.

I went home that night and couldn't sleep. All I wanted to do was talk to God and thank him for such an incredible new experience of him. And then I started thinking about my youth and all those days I went to Mass and why I had never felt like this before. Didn't I understand Mass back then? Had it only been routine? And in my prayerful thoughts, I decided to open the Bible randomly and read the passage on the page I landed on.

It was the parable of the two debtors (Lk 7:37–50). Jesus was in the middle of a debate about forgiving the woman who had anointed him and kissed his feet. The Pharisees couldn't understand that behavior, so Jesus had to explain to them that those who are forgiven more, love more. All of a sudden, everything made sense. That was me, too, in front of Jesus. I had spent so much time feeling unworthy of God and doubting that he would forgive my ten-year absence, that when he did, I felt tremendous waves of intense love for him. All these emotions that I couldn't contain translated into tears. I felt love for being forgiven what I thought was unforgivable. It almost seemed that all of my years away from the Church and my being lukewarm and outright hostile to God and the Church were necessary in order to experience the unimaginable forgiveness of God's infinite love for me.

I couldn't wait to call my mom and tell her my overwhelming experience of God at Mass. I didn't know how I would explain it to her, but I imagined I would use the words "love" and "forgiveness." When she answered, I just started talking about how happy I was, like a little kid telling his mom how he found a new friend on the first day of school. Finally there was silence. I could picture my mom smiling. When she spoke, she said, "That is all so good, but don't stop going to Mass."

Why would I stop going to Mass now? I couldn't wait to go to Mass every day! Did she think I would go back to my former life and forget about God again? There was no way that would happen to me. Not now, not ever. And I did go to Mass for many days in a row. Each day the tears would flow from the moment the priest appeared in the sanctuary. Some of the parishioners seemed annoyed with me. One day, two women who were in the pew in front of me started talking in Spanish to each other, not knowing that I could understand them. *"¡Oh no! ¡Aquí viene el llorón!"* which means, "Oh no! Here comes the crying baby!" It didn't even bother me. In fact, it made me smile because I could only think about how much God loved me.

The days went by, and I wish I could say that every single time I went to Mass, I felt like angels were singing next to me and the floods of tears and emotions were shaking me to my core, but my feelings started to change. One day I was late for Mass and totally indifferent to it after I arrived. Another day I didn't feel like going at all. I started excusing myself because I was tired after work or because I had many things to do. Some other days I felt bored, as if Mass were merely a lecture. I even left early a few times. The same way my deep emotions had come suddenly when I first began to attend Mass, apathy quickly started to take over my routine.

I had to call my mom and tell her I was afraid that I had lost my faith and love for God. But Mom really did know something I didn't. She said bluntly, "This is why I told you not to miss Mass. Feelings come and go, but I knew that there would be other days when you would feel bored at Mass or wouldn't even want to go. Those are the days that count the most because it is then when you can show God how much you really love him."

My mom knew that part of the journey very well. She knew I would fall, but she knew that when that moment came, I would need to make a free decision to love God even when I didn't feel him or when it seemed he wasn't even there. God wrapped his arms around me and kissed me every time I went to Mass. That was true whether I felt it or not.

Before ending our call, Mom asked, "Should we pray?" I really didn't feel like it, but after her amazing speech, I simply said, "Of course, Mom. Let's pray." And we prayed one decade of the Rosary. After that day, I am convinced that a new path in my journey opened up, and Mom knew exactly the possibilities that were ahead of me. She knew me very well as her son, but she also knew God very well too.

When you are in this part of your journey to the Father's house and find your participation at Mass wavering a bit, you are not alone. I say this not only because of my deeply fluctuating experiences as I returned to faith, but also because the same moments happen to me now as a priest. I know that for many people Mass is boring, or they can't understand it, or it's just another activity done during the week. I wish I could always experience how amazing it was for me those first few weeks of returning to Mass when I felt like someone who found a treasure. But the reality is I don't feel like that every day. We are consumed by so many things in this world. We are used to constant gratification and are driven by fast-paced stimuli. Unless we enter Mass as if it were a new experience or a new a treasure every time, it is very likely we will feel bored or nothing at all.

This is what we need when we approach the holy sacrifice of the Mass regardless of what we feel that day, whether we are tired, apathetic, or even bored. Take time before Mass to meditate on what it means to experience and to be at home in the Real Presence of Christ. Take time to recognize whatever feelings you have that day and give them to Christ: joy freedom, anxiety, anger, love, peace, and much more. Don't give up because you don't experience intense joy and love every time you go to Mass.

I must admit that when I feel tired or sleepy or upset about something, I enter Mass with a self-absorbed attitude. I feel bothered by everything. But what better place to be than with God himself? Check all your feelings before Mass begins and then let them go. If you do get distracted by your own feelings, that's OK too. Offer your distractions to God along with your love again and again. It's easy to love when we feel amazing. No credit for that. But loving when things are not so easy requires a purer love—one worthy of the Father who loves us.

Also, perhaps you know someone who is having a hard time going to Mass after a long time away from church. The prayers, the rituals, the constant movement from standing to sitting to kneeling, can be overwhelming. Don't give up on that person. Even if you don't know the answers to many theological questions about the Eucharist, accompany that friend to Mass. Bring your friend to God.

Prayer of a Prodigal

Thank you, God.
Because when I expected
Your anger,
You kissed me.
When I expected
Your condemnation,
You forgave me.
When I expected
Your rejection,
You put your arms around me.
When I expected your punishment,
You healed
My open wounds.
When I expected nothing,
You ran to embrace me,
And in tears
My heart found rest in you.
And now I know
That when you are my everything,
I am free.
Amen.

11

FOR THE LOVE OF GOD

"This son of mine was dead and is alive again."
—Luke 15:24

Words are often empty, their meaning carried away, it seems, with the wind. Actions, after all, really do speak louder than words. I was there, right on that thin line, wanting to fully express my deep love for God, to tell the world of his forgiveness and love for me.

I noticed some of my friends and coworkers behaved differently around me after *seeing* how I had changed, not after *hearing* how I had changed. And what was I supposed to do anyway? Go from door to door telling everyone how I found God and how much he loved me? Buy Bibles and give them to people in the streets so they, too, could find the treasure I had? Things like that always made me cringe. I didn't want to be one of those people who found religion and had to push it into everyone else's life.

I was stuck. But the idea of "more actions and fewer words" didn't vanish just because I didn't know what to do.

Instead it grew more powerful every day. It was a constant tug on my conscience, and I couldn't stop looking for situations and ways to do more. At first I started going to different churches to ask if I could help with something. Now I realize a strange man full of enthusiasm asking random people around a parish to take me into their community to help is weird. I, too, would have been wary of me. Nevertheless, not getting any positive response was discouraging.

In fact, I didn't know many people in the "business of God" that I could approach about how I might be of help. Yes, I could ask my mom, but my situation in a big foreign city was totally unfamiliar to her. I had to tell someone, though, so I eventually called Mom. As always, she listened and understood what I was feeling.

The surprising thing about this is that my mom's story was not at all like mine. She was always a devout Catholic. She never abandoned the Church for ten years to live a wild life somewhere far away. She never stopped praying or loving God. And yet, she felt the same subtle tug that made her want to do more. After I told her my story, she told me that with our recent conversations, she, too, had started to feel a deeper connection with God. She started talking to her friends and people who came to visit her about God and his love, mercy, and forgiveness in ways she had not done before. She said that it felt almost as if she was becoming a missionary.

That was the word I was looking for: *missionary*. But I always thought that missionaries were people who went to faraway countries and usually ended up martyrs. But my mother was onto something, and it just happened, without her searching for anything. She didn't have to go anywhere.

She could do more right there in her hometown and mostly without ever leaving her house.

A short time later, outside a local convenience store, a homeless man asked me for some cash. On my way into the store I said, "No," but when I came out, he said something that made me stop. "For the love of God, please give me some spare change." *For the love of God.* That sentence might not have meant anything to me in the past, but then it was a punch in the gut. Maybe this was the opportunity I had been looking for, my chance to do something more for the love of God.

I turned around, happy to have found a way to do something good, but as I got close to him, the odor around him was so strong that I threw money at him and ran back to my car. Yup. I did that. I drove home in shame and disappointment, but I couldn't go back. His odor was stronger than my good intentions. Of course I called my mother and told her what had happened. She then said something I already knew: "You always say that it would have been amazing to be an apostle of Jesus: to live with him, to touch him, to wash his feet, and to be with him. Well, you don't have to wish for that anymore. Jesus is really that man, and he is asking you for help. You need to look at it that way."

I returned to the store the next day, but the man wasn't there. I knew that I would eventually see him again. In fact, I had seen him there many times, so I just waited in my car. After a while, he showed up. Like a nervous little kid, my heart started thumping. I approached him slowly, and before I could get to him, he asked, "Do you have some change?" I was relieved that he didn't hold a grudge or even remember me, so I got closer this time. The smell was overpowering, and he was very dirty, but I managed to hand him some money. He smiled at me and, without hesitation, he stood up and hugged me for what seemed an eternity. At first I wanted to run like the day before, but it was as if my feet were nailed to the ground. After a few seconds, I hugged him back. I drove home in great joy. I still wanted to jump in the shower, but the feeling of doing something for the love of God surpassed any other emotions. For ten years, I had been dead inside. That day, I came alive.

I saw John almost every day after that, gave him some money, or bought him something to eat. Even though he always insisted that I sit with him for a bit, I always found an excuse not to. I knew in my head that loving God could not be reduced to just one simple gesture and that it was really a lifelong commitment, and that I needed to take the next step of sitting with John and getting to really know him. Just like with prayer and going to Mass, some deeds were going to be more difficult because they weren't accompanied by a feeling of "wow."

One day I gave John some money, and he just returned it. I thought he didn't need anything that day, so I insisted that he take it for later. "I don't want money today," he said. "I just want you to listen to some poems I wrote. Would you do that?" And for the first time without hesitation I said, "Yes." Then he pointed to a place on the curb and I sat next to him—too close for my sense of smell and germaphobia. For the next hour, he told me many stories about his life and read poems and even a movie script that he had written. When he was finished, I said to him, "John, do you mind if we pray together before I go?" His eyes opened wide. "Yes, please. When I was a child, my mother used to pray with me.

She was Catholic so she prayed the beads, but I forgot how to do it." "Don't worry," I said. "I will teach you." And just like my mother did with me a few months before, I taught John how to pray the Rosary. Before I left, I gave him a rosary that my mother had given to me. It was the only religious thing I'd kept for the past ten years, and I was attached to it because I thought that rosary was somehow miraculous. In that moment, I knew I didn't need it anymore. John did, and he took it as if it was a treasure.

That day was a great gift to me. I saw Jesus in a situation that made me uncomfortable. That encounter trained me for many future moments of seeking and finding God. My journey had opened me up to being transformed by God's presence, but also to being a signpost of God's love for others. The new life I had received, I could now give. That was my missionary way.

———

You might well find yourself wanting to do more for God. In fact, if you are like I was at this stage of your journey to the Father, you will sense that internal tug and pull that asks you to live your faith with more than just words. Don't give up if you get lost or if situations are not what you expected. The most amazing things happen when we allow ourselves to just be with God and become aware of everything we can do for love of him.

Your mission to bring God happens in daily life: at work, with your family, with your friends, during sad moments and celebrations. Prayer is important and should never stop, but actions in service of God should transform us. We find ourselves wanting to do more without expecting some kind of reward in return when we give our love to God freely and in every situation.

You might know someone who is ready to take this wonderful journey of turning prayer into actions. Know that they will find the same obstacles and questions I encountered. I realized that one of my main difficulties was that I was mostly alone. At that point, I didn't have any religious friends to accompany me, to show me what loving God could look like. Perhaps you are that companion, one that will support a friend through this fragile early stage of following God with enthusiasm.

We make it so complicated, but following God is actually easy. But there are things we have to do. We can't pray for things to happen, for us to be transformed, and then just sit comfortably at home or in a chapel. God did not rescue us from death so we could spend our new life with him relaxing on a sofa. Being good doesn't just happen because we desire it. We must put our faith into practice. Be there for someone who needs your support, and practice being good and holy together—for the love of God.

Prayer of a Prodigal

God,
I know I am nothing,
But in your eyes I am everything.
I know I fall,
But in your arms I am safe.
I know I was dead,
But in You I live again.
I know I am far away from loving as I should,
But you love me more than anything.
I will try again tomorrow
To be your hands, your eyes, and your heart,
So I can love others
The way you love.
Amen.

12

A GENTLE TORNADO

*"Quickly, bring out a robe—the best one—and put
it on him."*
—Luke 15:22

No journey back to God is finished the day it starts. As I
started getting to know God, I was guided through many
twists and turns. These variations in the journey are very
important in everybody's vocation. God's call to love him and
our neighbors is not a passive call. It is a movement with the
reality that we are made for eternity with God. Even though
I was happy with my progress in the spiritual life and the way
I was being transformed, I could never have foreseen the new
paths in my vocation.

Vocation was a familiar word to me. After all, when I was
eleven, I had decided to enter seminary. I was young then
and probably wasn't sure what being a priest really meant.
All I knew was that the priest in my little town was the most
amazing person I had ever met. Naturally, as we grew older,
many of us wanted to be like him, so five of my friends and I
decided to pursue the adventure of priesthood. Even though

minor seminary had a military feel and form to it, those six years were the best of my young life.

When I left the seminary, I didn't abandon God. I just didn't want to be a priest. I started focusing more on myself, on what I liked to do and where I wanted to travel. I went to different places in the world and finally ended up in Los Angeles, where I disconnected from God completely. But Los Angeles is also where God's love found me, the place where my journey back to the Father began.

On this journey home, the word *vocation* appeared again. It didn't scare me at first, because I remembered that *vocation* was literally defined as a call for *all* people to love and serve God. But one day, as the Mass began, I didn't connect with any emotions like sadness or deep joy but became extra attentive to the movements of the priests. It felt as if I was watching with my childhood eyes. In a flash, I remembered my seminary days and how much I had loved the idea of being a priest. Combined with how much love I felt from God in my adult conversion, I had a strange urge to be close to the altar. When the homily came, I had to gather all my strength to not run up there and tell the priest to move away so I could tell everyone how amazing God has been in my life, how much he has forgiven me, and how he had waited all this time for me with open arms. I wanted to stand before the people at Mass and tell them that God loved them just as much.

Honestly, this very vivid feeling frightened me. It made me feel like I had committed a sin. How could I, a sinful prodigal son, even think about taking the place of a priest? Who was I? Certainly not a priest. "And why can't you be one?" my inner voice whispered. Suddenly I couldn't move.

Frantic thoughts flooded my mind. For one thing, I was old. I was also a big sinner just coming out of my pigsty. It was impossible that people would accept a priest like that. God even less. Why was I even thinking about that?

Yet for the next several weeks, priesthood was all I could think about. I started praying about this not because I wanted it, but because I was trying to convince myself and God that the idea was ridiculous. Yet the idea of priesthood never went away. It was like a gentle tornado. God had already put the call in me, but very gently. After a while, and even without realizing, I started imagining my life as a priest. And little by little, I envisioned what priesthood would be like as a lifestyle, leaving God out of the mix completely.

This idea of imagining the lifestyle of a priest was so fragile, I kept on going back and forth with pros and cons. My age was a big issue, I thought. They would never take a thirty-three-year-old guy who had been out of the church for ten years. I had zero parish affiliation. I didn't know any priests who could vouch for me. Most of all, I didn't have any theological or liturgical training.

But while I knew that I couldn't make this happen, I realized that God could. Knowing that priesthood was impossible for me, I told God that if he wanted it, he would have to do the work, not me. So I stopped thinking so much about logistics and just prayed about the idea of priesthood, expecting that it would go away on its own. However, I did do some work. I got on my computer to see if there was a seminary in Los Angeles. There was, and it looked entirely different from the very structured minor seminary I had attended in Spain. Then I looked at costs. If it was too expensive, I couldn't consider it. It was free. I searched for an age limit. If it was under thirty, then I wouldn't qualify. There was no age limit. As I approached the end of the basic information page, I read, "If you are thinking about becoming a priest, contact this number and we can help you with your vocation." I slammed the laptop closed.

Naturally I reopened the laptop and stared at that phone number on the website for quite some time. Then I closed the laptop again. I debated whether or not to call the number for several days, all the time arguing with God about why I shouldn't. I needed to convince him to take away this vocation. But he never did. Next I was imagining being a seminarian, and I could picture the places that I saw in the photos on the website. I could see myself going into the beautiful chapel to pray and walking in those luscious gardens. I thought about what it would be like dining with the seminarians and using the library to study. The seed was already growing, and even though I didn't want to, I was already watering it.

After a few weeks, I decided I really did need to talk to someone about this. But who could I talk to? Maybe I could use that number on the website that I had already memorized? After all, it said that someone could help me with these thoughts. So, I bargained with God again. I would call that office on a Friday night at seven o'clock; if nobody was there to answer, then priesthood was out of the question. I thought I had a foolproof plan to avoid the priesthood.

Friday came, and I was nervous all day long. I was nearing the end of this beautiful nightmare. I paced and paced in my apartment, and when seven o'clock arrived, I picked up the phone and dialed. There was one ring tone, a second, then a third. I hadn't thought about how many rings should be part of my deal with God. Fourth ring tone. Fifth ring tone. OK, that was it. But as I was about to hang up, someone picked up the phone.

"Hello. This is Sr. Kathy." I closed my eyes and couldn't talk. "Hello," she repeated. I thought about hanging up, but instead I said, "Hello." Now I was in deep trouble. After I told her my name, we started to talk. She told me that she was closing her office door and leaving when she heard the phone. Usually, she would have let it go to voicemail, but for some reason, she went back and answered.

We talked for two hours. I told her my entire story, my conversion, my fears, my hesitations, and what seemed to be a call to priesthood. I was still hoping she would tell me that I was too old, or that I didn't belong to a parish, or that my sinful past meant I wasn't welcome. Instead she told me that this was meant to be. She said she was so happy that she had answered the phone. She invited me to a weekend of discernment at the seminary the following weekend. She mentioned that I wouldn't be alone; thirteen other men would be there. My vocation and an entirely new journey had just begun.

I am not sure if you have ever had some thoughts about becoming a religious or priest. I know those options can be scary. My initial response was not a good one. First, I tried to figure it out alone and on my terms. Second, I wanted to make it fit into what I wanted. So, I focused too much on material things—what I would lose or gain. I thought of me, me, me, and I left God out of the equation. My fears and expectations gave me unnecessary anxiety, and I forgot to pray or even ask for help. I found peace and clarity when I surrendered and let God take over.

Many prodigals who return to faith have similar experiences. You might be in the middle of this same dilemma, wondering about your worthiness for religious life. Personally, I wish I had heard the word *discernment* when I heard the call to priesthood. Discernment is a process of discovering what God wants for your life. We all need a way to discover if our call is really to priesthood, religious life, married life, or the life of the single laity. To talk with a vocation director (like Sr. Kathy) and to meet other people who are on the same journey was so important for me, and I am sure it would be for you too.

You might know someone who is thinking about religious life or priesthood who might need a little whisper and help in their discernment. Pray for this person first, and then invite him or her to pray with a community of people at your parish. Vocations are not made in solitude but in the community. If I'd had that kind of support, I would have avoided many fears and speculations.

Priesthood and religious life are beautiful gifts. But the most important vocation is the one we all have: to be holy, to be good, to love God above all things, and to love others the way God does. That's the starting point. Keep following a daily plan to anticipate how to be holy in whatever happens to you. Then let God do the rest. He knows better than we do, and in the end, he is the one doing the calling. When I accepted the fact that I wasn't worthy of the call, God gave it to me anyway. He takes sad and weary prodigals and dresses us in the finest robes. His love makes us worthy.

Vocation Prayer

Lord, give me the strength and the humility
To say yes to following you
Wherever you lead me.
I offer you my fears, my anxiety, my doubts,
And my uncertainties.
I give you all my attachments to this world.
All I can do now is place myself
In your hands
And trust you.
Help me to embrace the journey
Where I can love you the most,
Because I know that no matter what,
My vocation is love.
Amen.

13

A DIFFICULT ROAD

"Put a ring on his finger and sandals on his feet."
—Luke 15:22

The orientation retreat at the seminary was different from what I expected. I wanted to find reasons to say no to seminary life but found out that all my worries and obstacles were totally removed. This thing was becoming more real by the hour.

I went home after that weekend so full of joy and energy. I couldn't stop thinking of how my life would be on a daily basis if I lived there. I could almost feel the peace already. And the best part: there were two chapels, so I could spend more than my usual three hours in prayer. I could do this seminary thing, I thought. It looked so easy.

When Monday arrived, however, I realized I would have to tell everyone I knew about going to seminary to become a priest. I became nervous again. It had been hard enough to tell my friends about my new life as a Catholic, and it took time for them to accept it and not think that I was brainwashed. This would be even more difficult. "They will think I am crazy," I worried. I started having minor anxiety attacks overthinking things. I decided to do something I usually forgot when I was in a panic: talk to God.

I prayed constantly and waited several days before breaking the news to anyone. I didn't get the clarity and reassurance I prayed for. No angel came to me in dreams to tell me that everything would be fine, that this was the right path and everyone would be happy for me. I wasn't even sure that God was in favor of my decision. Nothing happened. No inspiration. It was me, God, and our silence.

I was very nervous, but, in prayer, I came to understand that it wasn't because of the news I was going to share. Really, becoming a priest was not completely out of this world. In prayer, I realized that I cared too much about what people thought of me. I was focused too much on myself and possible outcomes. Once again, I was leaving God out of the equation. Prayer helped me see that and take a step in a different direction. I decided to tell everyone and let God do his thing. Whatever the outcome, I would be happy even if I didn't understand it. Before I started making phone calls, I thanked God in advance.

Mom listened to my news, as always. I expected a huge celebratory cheer. Instead she remained quiet for a while and then said, "This is a big step. Being a priest is not just an adventure; it's a commitment to God and others. I don't want you to rush this or be taken by emotions. Have you found a spiritual director yet?" All this time I was so worried about myself that I had forgotten to find someone who could partner with me intimately and in whom I could share my deepest thoughts. I told Mom that finding a spiritual director was the next task on my list. We finished our conversation by praying together.

Telling Mom was easy. But I knew that my friends, the ones who already thought being religious was a bit weird, would not be so accepting of this news. There was no way back now. So, I asked a group of them out to dinner and planned to tell them all at once.

Some of my friends thought that I had snapped out of my "encounter with God phase" and was calling them so that we could go out and party like we used to. So, when I broke the news over dinner, they were confused. Why did I need to do that? Couldn't I be a good person in my job as a teacher? Did I need to leave behind all my things and my apartment? What if I didn't like being in seminary? Where and how would I start over again? So many valid questions, most of which I had already asked myself. I used the word *discernment*, and they ended up mostly tuning out. "Whatever. You do you." I knew that telling them was going to be painful, and it was.

Leaving everything and everyone behind was even harder. Every day was a roller coaster of emotions. Some days I was full of joy, but others I was filled with anxiety and sadness. I knew I needed to find a group of people to help me. I couldn't take these steps alone.

I called Sr. Kathy, the person who helped me over the phone. She told me there was a priest taking over the vocations office and I should talk to him. That's how I met Fr. Jim. Very soon after I met him, he started a First Fridays discernment group. It was great to meet with other guys who were going through many of the same obstacles and joys I was.

Fr. Jim was realistic and didn't judge my past or my many questions. He didn't paint the whole vocation picture as an easy ride. In fact, he was always very honest about the obstacles I was going to find, especially with my extroverted

personality and my desire to please people. He knew I needed time to work on that, so he asked me to stay in the discernment group for the next two years. At first I was a bit
disappointed. But part of me was also very happy. I had two
years to get my affairs in order, pay debts, get rid of things I
wasn't going to need, and prepare for a big change in my life.

It was very difficult to say goodbye to my neighbors. I had
lived in the same apartment for ten years and had become
very close to the two women who lived next to me. We all
had dogs and were each very extroverted, so against the norm
in LA, we became good friends. Every day after work, I used
to sit on the steps outside to decompress from the day. Then
we'd walk our dogs together. We never felt alone in a city
that suffers tremendously from loneliness. We knew we were
lucky to have found such friendships. Having to leave that
security and love hurt. The thought of leaving my dog behind
was more than I could bear. I had to find a solution to this.
I finally found a family who would take her. That goodbye
tore my heart apart as if someone had ripped it out of my
chest and stomped on it.

My neighbors were both from different religions, so I
thought it would be difficult to explain the priesthood to
them. As it turned out, they not only understood it; they supported me more than anyone else. As the time for me to go to
seminary drew closer, my neighbors helped me sell my stuff
and shop for new things I would need. When the moment
came, they accompanied me on my first day of seminary. I
will never forget that. Everyone had their families there that
day except for me, but these two wonderful friends filled
that spot.

I said goodbye to my coworkers and the job I had loved so much. Every step opened a wound, and I had to fight the doubts and fears that came. Part of me dreamed of going back to my pigsty and enjoying life the way I used to. And the closer to the big moment I got, the more intense the temptations became.

As I sorted out my material possessions, I found my attachment to them was stronger than ever. Every book, every movie, every piece of furniture I gave away felt like a bit of flesh was ripped from my heart. I had to say yes to my vocation every time I made a decision to leave something behind. It was spiritually and mentally exhausting, but I had support and I kept on going. Then, believe it or not, just weeks before my departure for seminary, several things happened to me. I got offered a better job, met the possible love of my life, and had the opportunity to make music with some famous people. All my worldly desires were aligning for me. It was very difficult, but I had to say yes to God one more time, and I did.

This journey was not easy. Just when I thought I had finished my way from the pigsty to the arms of the loving Father, another path opened up in front of me. It required me to pray, discern, trust, and be thankful to God regardless of the outcome. My mom always insisted that I never abandon prayer. In fact, she always reminded me that the more troubles and concerns that pass my way, the more time I should spend praying. I say the same to you. Do not abandon prayer. Do not abandon your calling. I know you might feel lost, and at times even God may seem very quiet. Those are the moments to draw closer to him. You need not worry about the future. God will put sandals on your feet for the road ahead. He will put a ring of his faithfulness on your finger.

Whatever vocation we follow will have many difficulties—especially as we approach times of decision. New opportunities to say no will come, and you will always face one more chance to freely choose your vocation. Trust that love and help will come from where you least expect it. God will give you friends who are more like family, ones who will not only pray *for* you and *with* you, but will always be there by your side. Now that I think about it, I am very glad that my road was difficult. The struggles helped me see how important my decision to enter the seminary was, and they showed me that God made this happen. I know for sure that it wasn't me. I wanted to give up so many times, but he put unexpected love on my path.

The journey to the Father's house cannot be made alone. It will bring doubts, fears, and regrets. If someone you know is walking this path, they are going to need you. They won't need you to explain anything or to cheer them up, but just to be there with them. All of us need someone who will not judge but will walk as far as possible with us, sharing the suffering and joy of vocation discernment. It changed my life to know that many people loved me and prayed for me. They showed up for me not only on my ordination day but all the days that followed. With the Father's ring on my finger and shoes on my feet, I had everything I needed.

Prayer of a Prodigal

Be with me, Lord.
Be patience when I am frustrated.
Be guidance when I am confused.
Be light when I am lost.
Be wisdom when I am uncertain.
Be my strength when I am weak.
Be my peace when I am anxious.
Be my joy when I am afraid.
Be my hope when I am lonely.
Be the ring on my finger.
Be the shoes on my feet.
Be the way I walk.
Be the home I seek.
Be with me, Lord.
Amen.

14

A LOVE LIKE THIS

*"Get the fatted calf and kill it, and let us eat
and celebrate."*
—Luke 15:23

I had already given my two-week notice for work and cleared
out my apartment. I knew I was going to sleep on the floor
the night before I drove to the seminary. I had a feeling that
I would love seminary and would do well there. I just had to
go through the last few days and hours before I could start
my new life. And the time came.

I woke up after barely any sleep. As I headed out, I had
to say goodbye to an apartment that had seen both my worst
and best moments. And in what seemed like a dream, it was
all gone. The past was now empty. I locked the door, dropped
the keys at my now former mailbox, and went to my car.

My first week in seminary was very different from what I
expected. It was orientation week and there were many new
things to learn. One of the hardest things for me to adjust to
was our super small rooms. Even after I got rid of 90 percent
of my stuff, I still had too many things. Some guys made
fun of me, but when I told them that this was all I owned,

their perspective changed. I had no family in the city where I could leave my books, clothes, or anything else. This was a very hard part of my journey because even though I knew I was too attached to things, I found it nearly impossible to get rid of some of my possessions.

Another hard realization was the idea that I wouldn't be as financially independent and secure as before. Even though I never got rich as a teacher, I never lacked anything I needed or most things I wanted. Now I had to budget. Even more difficult for me was living with a hundred other guys under the same roof. It was not what I had ever envisioned for my life, especially at the age of thirty-six. And I entered the seminary knowing that these would be my living conditions for the next seven years.

But there was one more thing I never expected to cause the most difficulties: it was me. My new way of living in the three years before I came to seminary had changed me, resulting in my intense prayer life and in my all-encompassing relationship with God. I had imagined seminary life being an extension of building an even deeper and more robust life of prayer, devotion, spiritual growth, and contemplation. I was surprised that it was not so. I had come from three hours of prayer a day, a constant awareness of the presence of God in my life, and an attitude of striving to be better. I accepted everything as the divine, loving, and perfect will of God. I understood the Bible better than I ever imagined that I would unless I took classes. My conversations with friends were mostly about love, peace, conversion, prayer, and God. I had a personal relationship with God, and I was proud and happy about it. Seminary was supposed to be the next step forward. But things didn't start that way, and sadly I was to blame for much of it.

Being in a moment of consolation and ease with God is wonderful, and I had enjoyed learning the good habits of prayer and closeness to God in every moment of my life. I was moved by love. It seemed so easy. My time was my own, and I could do what I wanted, which was to be in prayer. At the seminary, in just one blink of an eye, I lost it all. I went back to being stingy with my prayer time, to caring about what people thought of me, and to carrying a constant self-conscious embarrassment for being so extroverted.

My first year in seminary was trying in a lot of ways. I remember going to a small chapel during sleepless nights and placing myself under two cold marble columns that held a dark tabernacle to cry. I was so lonely and so lost. Had I made a mistake? Could I love God outside of a vocation to the priesthood? I was praying less and feeling less. My happy personality and positive disposition were crushed, and my extroversion seemed a curse. I remember making the most difficult prayer I had ever prayed: "Please, God, make me like all the others. Make me quieter, more introverted, so they will like me. Please, God, change me so I won't suffer." It was very painful, and all I heard was silence. I felt trapped as if in a different kind of pigsty, one with no exit. Is this what living in the house of the Father was supposed to be like? Did God bring me close to him for this?

In this time of complete spiritual solitude, my devotion and love for Mary blossomed again. I needed my mother. Phone calls weren't enough, so Mary was there to bring me consolation and walk with me. She was the support I needed when God seemed so quiet. I started praying the Rosary again, and at every Hail Mary I felt consolation and hope, so I abandoned myself to Mary's care. It was through her that I met again the gentle but firm Father who was with me in this new chapter of my ongoing pilgrimage.

Just when things began to settle down for me in seminary, my mom was diagnosed with cancer. It seemed as if every time I stood up to walk my path, something else happened that made me stop and fall to my knees. My dad had died recently, and this news was devastating. I went home for summer vacation, and things were not looking good. Mom underwent a serious surgery when I was there, and the time I thought I'd have to recharge became sleepless nights at the hospital with Mom. When she was discharged, it was time for me to go back to school. Just when I thought the worst was over, my sister called to tell me that Mom was dying.

I got home in time to kiss her. I knelt next to her bed for the next twenty-eight hours, singing and praying her favorite devotions. It was a chance to accompany her on the wonderful pilgrimage of dying to a new life, just as she had accompanied me on my return to God. Two days later, she died in my arms, peacefully, in the middle of praying the prayers she had learned from her own mother. While she was in my arms, I remembered my childhood, her love, her smiles, her constant teaching about God. It was almost as if she had waited for me to make my way back home to God so I could understand what Mom had always understood: our lives are made for God, and we are always on the journey.

The death of my mother changed my world forever. I will never be the same. I do not ever want to be the same. I felt alone, completely alone. The winds were quiet, the fire extinguished; my throat felt mute, and I could not sing again. I only felt silence in my heart. But in this silence, I felt God.

As my sister and I cleaned her house, everything was full of her presence. When we found her rosaries, numerous books, and prayer cards, my sister and I smiled. We knew that she had put us on the right path, and we did not feel sadness anymore but joy. Her aroma and laughter filled the house. I could hear her voice and feel her kisses. I sensed the Communion of Saints and the real hope for an eternal life. I became more aware of the present moment. It was as if I needed her death to experience what life really was. My prayer changed again, and my vocation did as well. I discovered the priest who brings the soul home to God. The priest whose mission is to be a signpost for pilgrims on the journey.

I came back to seminary with all of these thoughts wrapped in a broken heart, ready to share and explode with feelings. I wanted to be understood and listened to. But the world did not stop because of my pain. Everyone moved like they did before, while I was going in slow motion, waiting for hugs and understanding eyes. I got nothing. And then I surrendered.

How wonderful is our God, how much he loves us in the midst of our free choices, and how much he manifests his tenderness when we hurt the most! All we have to do is surrender, and he will come like a whispered breath. I knew all the theories of accepting the Cross, dying to oneself, trusting in God, hoping with humility, and that everything has a deeper meaning, but none of that was present in my heart when pain shook me to the core.

It took my mom's death for me to understand that life is abandonment and surrender to the sometimes inexplicable will of God. My connection with Mom, especially at her death, led me to a deeper union where my experience of sadness became spiritual, mystical, and metaphysical experiences. All of this led me to take the next steps in my relationship with God and with others. We are in constantly changing and improving states of life. Mom taught me this. She trusted that her love for God in her daily life would take her back home to the Father. She knew that prayer and devotions, absent an attitude of change and actual transformation in daily life, did not mean much. Being alone before God was the moment that Mom loved most.

My mother's death broke me into a million pieces, and at the same time it made me breathe again. Seeing my mother's life disappear in my arms was the most painful and peaceful thing I have ever experienced. All I could think was "What have I done to deserve a love like this?" I saw my life and how my mother was always there waiting for me. No reproaches. No questions. Just love. I realized that God had done the same thing for me. And then I asked God, "What have I done to deserve love like this?"

All the steps in this journey—the pain of detachment, the loneliness, the loss of family—all of these were not only important but necessary for my way back to God. These moments helped me realize that no matter what I do, none of this is about me or because of me. It's not because I am a strong person, but because God was always with me, even when I was far away from him. It was important for me to surrender, to abandon myself to the moments I didn't understand. My trust, hope, and faith were growing—not overnight and not because I was special—but because I was practicing trust. God does not waste anything. He will make good use of it all.

None of us deserves a love like God's, but he gives it to us anyway. There are a hundred thousand reasons to kill the fatted calf, to eat, and to celebrate. We all have so much to be grateful for. But above every other cause for joy is the Father, who not only waits for us to return to him but helps us take each step along the way. God does not give up on his children. It does not matter how far away we move from him. He stays with us and surrounds us with the love that leads us home. Here's to the journey that ends in his arms!

Prayer of Thanksgiving

I want to abandon myself to you, Lord,
Not only when I feel joy and peace in my journey,
But especially when I feel nothing
And I can't say much,
When I am tired or there is chaos around me.
I want to surrender my anxieties, my fears,
My pains, my desires,
And all that distracts me away from you.
I want to entrust my life completely to you
Because it is only in trust that I can
Express my love for you.
I thank you, Lord, for seizing my hand
When I thought I was sinking.
I thank you for receiving me
With open arms
When I thought I could not be forgiven.
Thank you for finding me
When I was lost and far away.
Thank you for giving me new life
When I was dead,
And food
When I was dying of hunger.
Help me to journey with you every day,
And as I spend time with you in prayer,
Show me how to love you more
By loving all you have created.
Lord, you know I am broken.
And I know that I could leave you again.
Sometimes my fears get the best of me
And I am tempted to return to darkness.

But I know that you will always be
Waiting for me
With open arms,
With a robe and ring I will never deserve,
Ready to kill the fatted calf
After a long embrace.
Amen.

Fr. Goyo Hidalgo is a priest in the Archdiocese of Los Angeles, a singer-songwriter, and a social media evangelist.

A native of La Villa de Don Fadrique, a small town near Toledo, Spain, he attended minor seminary as a youth to become a priest, but left after six years. He earned master's degrees in English and Spanish linguistics from Complutense University of Madrid in 1996, after which he traveled to other countries to teach Spanish and English. He eventually became a middle and high school teacher in the Los Angeles, California, area and released two albums of Catholic music in Spanish and English.

Hidalgo underwent a radical reversion to the faith of his youth after watching the funeral of Pope John Paul II in 2005 and hearing his famous words: "Do not be afraid."

Hidalgo earned a master of divinity degree from St. John's seminary in Camarillo, California, and was ordained to the priesthood in 2016.

Facebook: Fr. Goyo Hidalgo
Twitter: @FrGoyo
Instagram: @frgoyo